"We live in a time when many churches are anxious over scarcity. Here is a book to turn that paradigm inside out and upside down, like the gospel itself. Michael Mather shares his journey as an urban pastor through decades of personal and communal transformations that challenge stale assumptions about want and plenty. With humility and generosity, Mather shares an abundance of hard-won insight, helpful ideas, and inspiration for church leaders longing to approach their work with fresh eyes and to flourish in unforeseen ways."

— HEIDI NEUMARK
author of *Breathing Space: A Spiritual Journey in the South Bronx*

"In our times, many religious leaders suffer the despair of impossibility. The faithful seem trapped in the consumer culture, the church trapped by institutionalism. Nonetheless, there is a path to possibility. *Having Nothing, Possessing Everything* describes the adventures of a pastor who has walked that path. He discovers the gifts that surround him. He walks into the unknown, and the invisible becomes visible. He goes surrounded by neighbors—never alone. When you read this book, you will discover the joyful possibility of another way."

— JOHN MCKNIGHT
Northwestern University

Having Nothing, Possessing Everything

Finding Abundant Communities in Unexpected Places

Michael Mather

WILLIAM B. EERDMANS PUBLISHING COMPANY
GRAND RAPIDS, MICHIGAN

Wm. B. Eerdmans Publishing Co.
4035 Park East Court SE, Grand Rapids, Michigan 49546
www.eerdmans.com

Published 2018
Printed in the United States of America

27 26 25 24 23 22 21 20 19 18   1 2 3 4 5 6 7 8 9 10

ISBN 978-0-8028-7483-2

Library of Congress Cataloging-in-Publication Data

Names: Mather, Michael, 1959– author.
Title: Having nothing, possessing everything :
    finding abundant communities in unexpected places / Michael Mather.
Description: Grand Rapids : Eerdmans Publishing Co., 2018. |
    Includes bibliographical references and index.
Identifiers: LCCN 2018020963 | ISBN 9780802874832 (pbk. : alk. paper)
Subjects: LCSH: Broadway United Methodist Church (Indianapolis, Ind.) |
    Communities—Religious aspects—Christianity. |
    Wealth—Religious aspects—Christianity. | Church work. | Church.
Classification: LCC BX8483.I53 M38 2018 | DDC 287/.677252—dc23 LC record
    available at https://lccn.loc.gov/2018020963

Opposite page: Lucille Clifton, "in the inner city," from *The Collected Poems of Lucille Clifton*. Copyright ©1969, 1987 by Lucille Clifton. Reprinted with the permission of The Permissions Company, Inc., on behalf of BOA Editions Ltd., www.boaeditions.org.

in the inner city
or
like we call it
home
we think a lot about uptown
and the silent nights
and the houses straight as
dead men
and the pastel lights
and we hang on to our no place
happy to be alive
and in the inner city
or
like we call it
home

—*Lucille Clifton*

Contents

Foreword by Fr. Gregory Boyle   ix

*Preface: Finding Riches Where
I Had Thought There Was Nothing*   xi

1. Into the Inner City   1

2. Hidden in Plain Sight   14

3. Noticing People's Gifts   35

4. Getting Out of the Way   51

5. Making Sense of Money   60

6. Practicing Hospitality   77

7. Taking Learning Journeys   87

8. The Lights of Broadway   110

Epilogue: Two Things Became Visible   134

Afterword   139

Bibliography   141

Acknowledgments   143

Foreword

Something needs to be turned on its head.

Graduates get sent out every year to "make a difference" in the world, and yet, how is this venture then . . . NOT about THEM. We don't go to the margins to "make a difference." We go to the margins so that the folks at the margins make US different. We don't walk with the poor and the disparaged to rescue them. But— go figure—if we locate ourselves WITH them, we all find rescue.

Mike Mather invites us into the beauty of exquisite mutuality at the margins. The scales fall from our eyes as we no longer insist on the divide between "Service Provider" and "Service Recipient." We want to bridge even the space that keeps us from each other in service. At Homeboy Industries, a vicinity I've been privileged to occupy for over thirty years, I am not the great healer and that gang member over there is not in need of my exquisite healing. We are all a cry for help . . . we are all in need of healing. This is one of the very things that joins us together as we share our common humanity. When we discover that there is no longer daylight separating us from each other, we inhabit our mutual nobility and dignity, and everyone finds resonance in the line often uttered before Buddhist teachings: "O nobly born, . . . remember who you really are."

Our notion of service needs to find itself situated in an expansive, spacious notion of the God who loves us without measure and without regret. We allow ourselves to be reached by the tender glance of God and then feel compelled to be that tender glance in the world. This, of course, is where the joy is. Mike Mather knows this and shares this insight with us. As Jesus says, "My joy yours . . . your joy complete." Then the "widow, orphan, and stranger" guide the rest of us to the kinship of God such that God might recognize it. The fact that service is not, now, some grim duty, but rather a selfish endeavor meant to lead all parties to shared nobility, is a good and necessary shift.

Time to turn something on its head.

FR. GREGORY BOYLE

Finding Riches Where I Had Thought There Was Nothing

When I was nineteen years old, I was called to be a pastor. I had thought I was going to be a professional jazz trumpet player. And then, late in my first year of college, I found myself making a different choice. A very different choice.

In my calling as a pastor, I wanted to live and work in low-income parishes. I grew up in small towns in southern Indiana, and I loved those places. I wanted to spend more time in the city, though—not for the culture, the theater, and the bookstores, but because there were concentrations of poverty there, and I wanted to do something about that.

For the last thirty-one years, I've worked in two low-income parishes, one in South Bend and the other in Indianapolis, Indiana. The people of those parishes, inside and outside of the congregations, tolerated me, challenged me, loved me, and taught me.

What they taught me, most fundamentally, was a different way of seeing the world. I began my ministry seeing scarcity, seeing only the need and the things that seemed to be missing in the neighborhoods in which I pastored. What I learned from those among and with whom I worked in South Bend and Indianapolis was how to see abundance—I learned to see the love and power that was overflowing in even the most economically challenged neighborhoods. I began my work as a pastor committed to addressing the scarcity that I saw in the lives of the poor and the marginalized, and now I often feel overwhelmed by the abundance I see, riches where I had thought there was nothing.

This journey has often been painful, humbling, trying. But I've not been alone. My wife of thirty-seven years (at this writing), Kathy Licht, and our two sons, Conor and Jordan, have been not only constant companions, but also witnesses with their own lives of the abundance and joy that are always present. My journey so far has been well worth the challenges, and I imagine and expect that I will continue to grow and learn in this life.

I certainly hope you will find the stories, mistakes, and lessons contained in this book good fuel for your own growth and learning. But I want you to know at the outset that this book doesn't propose a model for the work of ministry, for urban ministry, or for any kind of work in low-income neighborhoods. There is no model, no replicable system to be imitated in community after community, no summons to multiply something that worked well somewhere else. The only thing being sold in this book is the invitation to pay attention to the wondrous children of God (especially low-income, low-wealth persons) around us and to the gifts they bring to the world.

The stories in this book, my own and the stories of people of our parish, are stories of disappointment, failure, death, and new beginnings. Grief is wound in and through these stories. But that's not all. They are also stories of change, hope, learning, and power.

I have learned more than a few lessons along the way. And I keep learning them. As I walk through those lessons, I have seen a few patterns emerge.

I now tune my eyes, my ears—all of my senses—and my heart to see abundance instead of poverty. I'm not successful all the time. But my re-tuning caused me to re-think how I spend my time. What will I lay aside, and what will I pick up?

I used to do things for people that people can in fact do for themselves. No longer. I expect more from people than I used to, and wonders pour forth.

1

Into the Inner City

Young people, from ages four to eighteen, gather outside the door to Broadway Church. It's lunch time, and they're waiting for the doors to open. They are a rollicking, joyous mass. Bodies push against one another, laughing, a hum of activity and life. The faces show differing shades of blackness: brown sugar, sepia, coal, smoke, and midnight.

As the lunch hour grows near, the bodies move even closer together. The crowd pulses and shakes. The crowd *is* energy. Individuals are blurry. Now a young woman with a knife is moving among them, but no one notices the glint of steel in her hand. She raises the knife, aiming at the back of the young woman in front of her.

Out of the chaos, another young woman sweeps into view. She holds a broom in her hands, and suddenly she is between the knife and its target. She moves the knife-wielding woman away from the crowd. She pushes her down the street. She is both hurried and deliberate. She's not going to turn away.

Who is this young woman with the broom? What possessed her to get involved in that fracas? She hears I'm asking about her, and she swoops into my office and throws herself into a chair. Exhausted, exhilarated, she says, "I'm going to be the next Martin

Luther King Jr.!" I believe her. She introduces herself. "I'm Seana Murphy. I live half a block up the street, with my parents and my sisters and brothers. Are you the new preacher?" Seana has an exuberant, confident smile, even with the sweat from the summertime heat and the encounter beading on her face. She is calm. In control. She is seventeen years old and a high school senior. She knows the young woman with the knife, has known her for years. "She'll be all right," she says.

More than two decades later, Seana tells me that the woman who'd wielded the knife is a good mom with a decent job and a quiet life. "Weren't you scared?" I ask, long after that tumultuous day.

"Of course I was," she says. "The whole time I was sweeping her down the street, I was praying, 'Please, God, don't let her push that knife down my throat. Please, God, don't let her push that knife down my throat.'"

Here it is—violence and destruction in the midst of life, and the people of this place in all their beauty and power. I've spent over thirty years of ministry at the intersection of violence and beauty, in the company of remarkable people like Seana and the woman with the knife.

Welcome to Indianapolis

In 1986, just one year out of seminary, I came to Broadway United Methodist Church in Indianapolis. Broadway's building was a cathedral. Its towering presence was evidence of the grandiose aspirations of those who built it. Many neighbors called Broadway "The White House" for the way it soared above the other buildings in our part of the neighborhood, for the complexion of most of the congregation, and for the quasi-governmental role, as a social service agency, it played in their lives. It took me three years to find my way, comfortably, around the immense building without

More than two decades later, Seana tells me that the woman who'd wielded the knife is a good mom with a decent job and a quiet life. "Weren't you scared?" I ask, long after that tumultuous day.

"Of course I was," she says. "The whole time I was sweeping her down the street, I was praying, 'Please, God, don't let her push that knife down my throat.'"

getting lost. In fact, I didn't spend much time in the building—my job at the church was as the pastor in the streets. I was appointed to oversee Broadway's outreach ministry in our inner-city neighborhood. Mrs. Miller, who lived down the street, called me "the hoodlum priest." My parish was the streets. In 1986 Indianapolis was a genteel city, caught between past glories and present uncertainties. It was also a city long on compassion but short on justice, as the senior pastor at Broadway in the eighties and nineties often said.

The neighborhood around Broadway—including the large homes once occupied by prosperous white families—was falling into disrepair, the result of age, little capital, and negligent landlords. Children played curb ball; they didn't have many other options. On nearly every block, concrete steps rose from the sidewalk to squares of grass and weeds, empty lots where houses had once stood, where families had slept peacefully in bedrooms overlooking the street, and where meals had been shared in kitchens and dining rooms.

Ninety years ago, the streets had been newly paved for the business people and teachers who walked from their homes, down their steps, and onto sidewalks shaded by the fruit trees the city had planted between sidewalk and street to entice their young professional class to move off the farm and into the city. The young people in those homes had walked to Broadway Church on Sunday mornings, some coming from just down the block and others crossing the College Avenue and Central Avenue bridges spanning Fall Creek and its adjacent parkway, the southern border of Broadway. In those years, the wide parkway, the flowing waters, the blooming trees—all spoke of promise and of the commitment the city had made to this place and these people. There were porches on every home—some houses even had porches on the second floor as well as the first. People expected to see one another.

The church moved to the Broadway location in the late 1920s, when this neighborhood, thirty blocks north of downtown, was the suburbs. On Sunday mornings in the 1940s and 1950s, cars double-parked on Fall Creek Parkway in front of the church, bringing young families to join in the swelling chorus singing the rising city's hallelujahs. The sanctuary, a cathedral, was full, with chairs set up down the center aisle to welcome the growing crowd.

As more and more black families moved into the neighborhood in the late 1950s and 1960s, what had once been a suburban white neighborhood became the black inner city. The pews emptied, and the streets held only scattered parked cars on Sunday morning. The rise and fall looked swift from my perspective. But those who remained told stories of years and years when the community room in the church was full of people eating together at church and community functions, and staging plays, talent shows, concerts, madrigals, and festivals that brought joy to their lives.

Things had changed. Those who remained at Broadway saw what was happening but felt powerless to do anything about it. They were grieving. A way of life they felt they understood was changing. Their neighbors and friends were leaving because black people were moving next door. Broadway members were leaving its pews for churches nearer their new suburban homes, and many of the members who stayed felt anger, confusion, and despair. For me, a young pastor arriving after the neighborhood and church

4

rolls had already changed, the stories I heard about Broadway seemed like the striations on the cliff walls I saw out West, revealing the eons that had passed long ago. But for many of the people at Broadway, the changes were an open wound.

In the 1980s, the hum of conversations between families on their front porches gave way to the deep, bone-rumbling beats of music booming out of cars filled with young men. The many children and teenagers who now filled the unrepaired streets and broken sidewalks eclipsed the relatively few children who had walked the streets decades before. In the 1930s and '40s, life on the then-white streets had filled the city with hope and energy. Two generations later, the young black and brown people on the streets outside Broadway filled the white city fathers and mothers with fear. The fruit trees were disappearing, almost all gone. And in their place were patches of brown matching the complexion of the new residents—the vanishing fruit trees a signal of the barrenness the city seemed to see when it looked at the new generation.

The parking lot for Broadway now served as a gathering place for young people. Young men played basketball (and sometimes football) there. A drill team of young women often lined up in the parking lot. The steady beat of the drill team's moves, punctuated by stomps, reverberated with the syncopation of the basketball popping off the asphalt and into young men's hands.

These same young people lined up to eat lunch in a basement room of the church or to quench their thirst at the water fountain. But only for special events did they make their way into the community room—and never into the holy space beneath the soaring ceilings of the sanctuary.

Broadway's congregation was predominantly white, aging, and liberal. Over the decades, the men and women of Broadway had developed the staples of white mainstream Protestantism's approach to urban ministry. There was a food pantry, a summer program for neighborhood kids, a tutoring program during the school year, and a giveaway of toys, food, and clothing at Christmas.

Part of my job, as the associate pastor, was to work with three other congregations whose members often volunteered in one or another of Broadway's programs. Philip Amerson, Broadway's senior pastor, created an innovative committee made up of a pastor and a layperson from Broadway and each of the other three congregations, along with a couple of representatives from the neighborhood. It was called the Broadway Community Project, and it was the group to which I was accountable. My job was to find ways to invite them into deeper relationships with the neighbors they were serving. I was to recruit more volunteers, both from the churches and the neighborhood, and to explore new ways of living and working together.

Am I the Savior or Something Else?

I thought I had been sent to Broadway to help. I would be Christ, or at least Christ-like, to the hurting, needy people of our neighborhood. I'd been trained for this work in seminary and raised on a vision of sacrificial helping from my earliest memories. Taking mission trips to Mexico with my parents, dropping coins into Sunday school collections for people in Taiwan, gathering up donations for a local food pantry—all these actions had taught me what it means to be a Christian, what it means to be a human, and what it means to be the church.

As the people I encountered through Broadway began to open my eyes to a new reality, I started to think that maybe I was also sent to Broadway to be a witness. Not only one who observes, but one who announces and testifies to what is happening. I was being invited to see the people—people I had once thought of as helpless—as powerful, brave people with both extraordinary and ordinary gifts. I was going to have to recalibrate my life, my work,

> It was called the Broadway Community Project,
> and it was the group to which I was accountable.
> Members of these other congregations often vol-
> unteered at Broadway's inner-city projects. My
> job was to find ways to invite them into deeper re-
> lationships with the neighbors they were serving.
> I was to recruit more volunteers, both from the
> churches and the neighborhood, and to explore
> new ways of living and working together.

and my practices if I was going to serve as more than a spectator, but not the lead actor.

I believe that sometimes I am called to act. But in living and working in churches in Indiana, I came to see that those times are rarer than I had imagined. I discovered that most of the time, the action needed from me was shining a spotlight on the glories of the people in our neighborhood. I also learned that I could act behind the scenes. As the leader of an institution, I could help organize our work in ways that invest in the good gifts of our neighbors, rather than treating them as needy or undereducated, or, worse, as drains on the church's resources. I could name the invisible beauty in the places of poverty: the gifts, talents, dreams, and passions—the abundance that is there to be gathered and celebrated and utilized in richly diverse ways.

At the Edge of a Knife

The rhythms that swept out of the cars in the street, the swells of the organ in the church building, and the language of the streets pouring out of young and old were teaching me a new song. But I wasn't grooving to it yet. I was still moving to the rhythms of scarcity. My ears were tuned to what was missing. My hands were busy pounding out songs that invited those in the congregation to join in helping people in their emptiness.

But Seana and the young woman with the knife were proof of something powerful and puzzling. In every community—even the communities that are home to those we good church people label as underserved and poor—live men, women, and children filled with power and grace. That's one of the refrains of the new song I was learning.

In seeing and recognizing the grace and power in Seana's life, I was beginning to understand my own gifts—and my own shortcomings. I wanted to be the do-gooder who was sent to the inner city—to "the least, and the last, and the lost," in the language of the church—to save and redeem. At the edge of a knife, in the brush of a broom, I began to see the power and agency in the people I came to serve. And I began to ask myself some important questions that shifted how I was seeing my calling, my work. What if I were to start treating the poor as if they were real people—people like me in every respect, except with less money? That would mean recognizing the abundance and power around me—and if I took that first question seriously, I'd hear it asking additional questions of me. I'd hear it inviting me to act in different ways, develop new practices, and tell stories from a different perspective.

I began to see that everyone around me wanted to be useful, to be needed, just as I wanted to be useful and needed. Whether it was a young man who sold drugs but wanted his sister to see him as a teacher, or a woman who worked hard every day to keep a roof over her children's heads and food in their bellies, or an elderly man who lived alone and paid attention to all the children on his street, especially ones he suspected were being abused—all those people wanted to be useful, just as I did.

At the edge of a knife, in the brush of a broom, I began to see the power and agency in the people I came to serve. And I began to ask myself some important questions that shifted how I was seeing my calling, my work. What if I were to start treating the poor as if they were real people—people like me in every respect, except with less money? That would mean recognizing the abundance and power around me—and if I took that first question seriously, I'd hear it asking additional questions of me.

I began not only to notice the gifts of people around me, but to find a place for them in the life of the community. The problem was that I had no set of practices to guide me. All my training had been in helping people in their need, but now their talents, capacities, passions, and dreams were bumping into me, looking for some way to be expressed, to be useful.

I was paid to run the church's programs for the poor, and sometimes I needed to pay others to keep the programs going. In my first years of ministry, I very rarely hired the poor themselves. Money flowed away from the neighborhood even though it was being used to serve the neighborhood. Slowly that turned around, and money began flowing into the hands of our neighbors.

I never liked school, but neighborhood ministry has been a continuous education. I learned from the wise elders in the streets and in their homes, from the young people in the parking lot, and from the church members at Broadway. My teachers were plentiful: Seana, the other pastors at the church, the old ladies in the pews, the young men who hung out on the street corners, the old men giving advice to the ball players on the court. I began to seek out other teachers: authors who wrote books I loved, economists who thought practically about low-income communities, and physicians who paid attention to the art of healing.

When I was preparing for ordination, a denominational official asked me what I needed to work on in my ministry. "I need to work on my risk-taking," I responded. Did I know what I was saying? Not likely. Across the years I have taken more risks than I imagined I would. And I'm still learning.

Expecting Miracles

My first steps in trying to help people were programmatic. Programs, I thought, held the solutions. I was, after all, a child of church programming—as a kid, I'd attended Vacation Bible School, Sunday school, and youth group.

And yet those programs—or, rather, the Scripture I encountered in them—taught me to expect something grander than felt boards and packaged curricula. At Vacation Bible School, I sang biblical songs, I learned biblical stories, and I played biblical games. The stories awakened something powerful in me. In these stories, a little boy, David the shepherd, could defeat Goliath the giant with a slingshot and one carefully placed stone. In these stories, miracles appeared like magic tricks—Moses parting the waters of the Red Sea to escape from slavery in Egypt, Jesus feeding five thousand people with only five loaves and two fish. These stories were amazing.

Now, not even fifteen years later, I was the associate pastor, running the outreach programs at Broadway Church in Indianapolis. My first responsibility was to oversee the summer program—which, at Broadway, was biblical only in its interminability. It wasn't at all like the VBS I had experienced growing up. In this summer program the young men were playing basketball, and the young women were serving as cheerleaders. The only thing

> My first steps in trying to help people were
> programmatic. Programs, I thought, held the
> solutions.

in the ballpark close to a Bible lesson was the rule against taking the Lord's name in vain that held sway on the court.

This was the best I could do? No waters parted, no food multiplied? The truth was, astounding miracles hadn't happened in the suburban and rural churches where I'd first heard miraculous Bible stories, either. But I expected to see something different in Indianapolis. The city was where the action was, where Jesus pulled off his miracles, where people were really needy, running for their lives or going hungry, lingering hopefully out on the mountainside.

The summer program wasn't bad, but its main virtue was that the staff, the congregation, and I were feeling good about providing the program. It was doing nothing to change the futures of the young people. In fact, during those years we didn't even ask ourselves if we were changing their futures; we just imagined that we were.

I was the supervisor of the summer program leaders, men I thought of as old (they were in their forties) who clearly had the respect of the young men from the neighborhood. They presided over the games with iron fists and gave careful instruction in the art of basketball. I talked with these leaders about expanding the offerings beyond sport. They said they were amenable to changes, but none of us took steps to increase the offerings. For two years, I was the associate pastor of summer basketball.

I decided I wanted to change the summer program so that lives would change. So, in 1987, with the support of the church staff and leaders and members of the congregation, I threw out the old program and created The Jubilee Summer Program. We built each week around a spiritual principle. We started every day with devotions; we ended every day with devotions. We divided the program into two parts: Recreation for a Healthy Body and Education for the Human Spirit. We offered swimming and tennis and basketball. We offered classes in Bible study, poetry, math, history, science, and violin. We took field trips to the Children's Museum, to the Indianapolis Zoo, and to the Indiana State Museum. Two hundred and fifty young people gathered every day, Monday through Friday, from nine a.m. to five p.m. This seemed like a miracle!

Most of the people in the church and the neighborhood around us felt great about the changes we had made. We got a lot of attention both in Indianapolis and beyond for what we were doing. I broke my arm patting myself on the back, I felt so good.

And Yet

And yet, what happened next changed me, my work, my ministry, and my life.

Forever.

Death. Nine young men in my last nine months as associate pastor in Indianapolis. Nine young men in the four-block radius around our church building. Nine young men in the full flower of their possibility. Nine young men struck down by violence.

Marvin and David and Jaguar were first.

Marvin was always willing to talk. He had no reason to talk to me, but he did. He carried his weight, like he carried his youth, lightly. He loved to laugh, but he was serious too. Everybody liked him, in life and in death.

David. Hard-as-marble David. Fierce and dangerous. He came to me once for shoes. "Good" shoes, he said. His infant son had died, and he wanted good shoes for the funeral. We found some. Standing at his casket, I wondered if the shoes were hidden, like the gentleness he rarely showed.

> What happened next changed me, my work, my
> ministry, and my life.

Jaguar. Jacques on his birth certificate; Jaguar on the strect. The others died by bullet. He fell by a knife. Both steel. Both deadly. Young men would gather around him on his porch. He listened, told stories, and gave advice. On the porch it could get loud—laughter and anger. Now it was quiet.

There were six more. Six more times singing "Amazing Grace." Six more times watching young men move toward the casket, trying to pull off swagger under the weight of grief. Six more times listening to the parade of preachers trying to shout down the violence, shame the young, and comfort the family.

In the same year, my colleague Philip Amerson introduced me to the sociologist Lisbeth Schorr. About the war on poverty, Schorr wrote that the question at the heart of that "war" was this: Is the work the government is doing helping a few people beat the odds or changing the odds for everyone? As I saw it, we were expending a lot of time and energy (and money) to see a few people do very well. And perhaps those young people were going to do well anyway. Phil was a huge influence on me, so when he raised Schorr's question, I paid attention. But what kept Schorr's question—which, whether or not she intended it as such, is a *biblical* question—before me were the bodies of those young men. The summer program, the food pantry, the tutoring program—all were helpful to a small number of people beating the odds. We had our success stories to tell. But we also had our funerals. Now I wanted to figure out if it was possible to change the odds for everyone.

2

Hidden in Plain Sight

At the beginning of 1992, my bishop appointed me to a church in South Bend, and I left Indianapolis. I moved to a very small congregation, but we did have a food pantry. We were known as the "social-service church" in our low-income neighborhood. When people came to the pantry, they were required to fill out a government form, because we received government surplus food. The form asked for their name, address, income, and expenses.

In worship on Pentecost Sunday that June, we read the passage from Acts 2 where Peter is preaching from the prophet Joel. Joel shares this word from God: "I will pour out my Spirit upon all flesh." After worship, around the table at the Sunday community dinner, we were talking about Joel's testimony, and an insightful woman said to me, "If what Joel said is true, why don't we treat people like that?" I asked what she meant, and she continued, "When people come to the food pantry, we ask people how poor they are rather than how rich they are. Peter is saying all people have God's Spirit poured into them."

I stopped. I didn't know what to say. Shamed, I whispered, "You're right." We were actually working against our beliefs. We say in worship that "God's Spirit flows down on everyone," and then we act like it isn't true.

That woman's question got me thinking about something called Asset-Based Community Development (ABCD). John McKnight and Jody Kretzmann, cofounders of ABCD, proposed that when working with low-income citizens, you ought to begin by focusing on the gifts of the community rather than starting with what the community lacks. Specifically, McKnight and Kretzmann urged communities—both the "helpers" and the ones "receiving help"—to notice the gifts of individuals, the gifts of associations, and the gifts of institutions. McKnight's *The Future of Low-Income Communities and the People Who Reside There* included a questionnaire designed to tease out people's individual gifts, and when our Pentecost Bible study shined a bright light on our church's failure to receive people as the gifts they are, I recalled the questionnaire. This led to an important change in how we interacted with the people who came to our food pantry. Now we began with those questions. We asked whether folks took care of children or elders, and whether they did it with their family or as part of a job or to help out a neighbor. We asked whether people could put up drywall or fix a toaster or knew how to drive a car. "Do you play a musical instrument?" we asked. "Do you garden?" If so, "Do you grow vegetables, flowers, or both?"

And each interviewer asked three more questions at the end of the survey:

1. What three things do you do well enough that you could teach them to someone else?
2. What three things would you like to learn that you don't already know?
3. Who besides God and me [the interviewer] is going to go with you along the way?

We asked the last question because when people came to the pantry, they seemed to be feeling isolated and alone. People often answered that question with some version of "There's no one."

1. What three things do you do well enough that you could teach them to someone else?
2. What three things would you like to learn that you don't already know?
3. Who besides God and me [the interviewer] is going to go with you along the way?

The interviewer followed up such an answer by asking, "Who celebrated your last birthday with you?" And as people named folks, they began to sit up, and you could see light come into their eyes. People remembered they weren't alone.

One of the first people who came to the food pantry after we began using this questionnaire was a neighbor, Adele Almaguer. Three generations of her family were living in her home, and she was working part-time at the University of Notre Dame as a cook. She told us she was a good cook, and we said, "Prove it." When she asked what we meant, we asked her to cook lunch one day for the custodian, the secretary, and the pastor (me). The lunch she prepared was fabulous.

Shortly after that, we heard that the leaders of the neighborhood organization were planning to meet at a restaurant. The church secretary told them, "Don't do that. Meet here at the church, and let Adele cook for you." They did, and they paid her for the meal. Over the next nine months, Adele catered three events in the neighborhood. Studebaker Elementary was holding a parent-teacher meeting, and she cooked for it. The Southeast Side Neighborhood Health Center held an open house, and she provided the food. Memorial Hospital held a press conference in our neighborhood, and she served refreshments to the reporters. Then the Chamber of Commerce contacted us. They wanted to have an all-day meeting of their leadership group in our church building. Since they were going to be there all day, they wanted to use the kitchen. We told them they could, but that we preferred they use our caterer. And they agreed.

We took twenty dollars (our only investment) and bought Adele a thousand business cards that said "La Chaparrita Catering: Spunky Tex-Mex Food." When she fed seventy of the business and civic leaders in the community, she put those cards to good use. She also got connected to the Michiana Business Women's Association, and a year and a half later she opened Adelita's Fajitas at the corner of 8th and Harrison in Elkhart, Indiana.

If we had asked Adele how poor she was, we would all have ended up poorer for it. We would also have missed a lot of great food. Adele taught us that if we asked different questions, we would discover a world of gifts we didn't know existed in people's lives, and we would see different results. If we began looking for people's gifts rather than people's needs, then even better things than we thought possible might materialize.

I had stumbled into an awakening. A revelation. We hadn't created anything. We hadn't taught Adele how to cook. She knew how to cook. We hadn't given her "life skills." She already had those. What we did was invest in *her*. We paid for her to share her gift, and then we found others who were looking for someone with that gift. We were practicing the theology of abundance by looking for and naming the gifts of people who are thought of as poor and needy. Throughout the Gospels, Jesus proclaims Good News to the poor. Likewise, our telling people who thought they had nothing to offer that they had gifts was indeed good news. And very effective.

If Adele had shown up two weeks earlier, we would never have asked her about her giftedness. The gift would have been there, but we would have missed it. We began to think that building on the gifts of people rather than filling their needs could hold the key to changing the odds for everyone.

> If we had asked Adele how poor she was, we would
> all have ended up poorer for it. We would also have
> missed a lot of great food. Adele taught us that if
> we asked different questions, we would discover
> a world of gifts we didn't know existed in people's
> lives, and we would see different results.

Back to Broadway

Over the next decade, I grew in ministry in South Bend, helping connect an inventor in our neighborhood with venture capitalists, and writing grants with neighbors who wanted to share their gifts in health and entrepreneurship and the arts. In 2003, I received a call from my bishop's office with mixed feelings—I was, the bishop said, being sent back to Broadway in Indianapolis, this time as senior pastor. It was hard—in some ways shocking—to leave the good folks in South Bend. I loved being there. But it was comforting to return to a familiar place. The size of Broadway's congregation and building and the form of mission were very different from South Bend, but it wasn't foreign territory, and I was glad about that.

When I went back to Broadway, much about it felt unchanged. There were, of course, some new members, but the character of the place was the same as it had been in the 1990s. Broadway was still a welcoming place to GLBTQI folks. The music program was still going strong. The neighborhood around Broadway had also changed very little in the last decade. Still, there were signs that gentrification was making its way toward us. Just south of the church, across from Fall Creek Parkway (one of the major thoroughfares from the northern suburbs to downtown, another two miles south of us), major redevelopment commitments by the city had brought new housing, renovated housing, and new neighbors with much higher economic status.

These new neighbors were often the focus of the conversations that congregants had about how the church might grow. They had been worried about the church's future since the late 1950s, when white flight started, and they saw the new neighbors as potential members. But this small number of new, white, more affluent people weren't pouring into the church, and that was worrying to the congregation. They felt that in order to be fully alive, they needed to return to the glory days of 1952. I felt my congregation's anxiety—it landed with particular force on the building. Would we be able to keep this expensive building open if we didn't grow dramatically?

Indeed, at almost every meeting of the congregation in the 1980s and again in the mid-2000s, the topic "How can we grow?" took up all the energy in the room. And the question "In what way are we as a congregation alive?" didn't occur to us. We spent so much time talking about what we weren't doing and what magic formula could turn things around that we weren't noticing what an exciting, vibrant parish we already were.

It gradually occurred to me that the inability to see gifts afflicted us not just when we looked at "the poor." It also afflicted us when we looked at ourselves. Just as the congregation in South Bend had, for a long while, missed the gifts of the men and women who came to receive services, the people at Broadway, pastor included, were so anxious about the congregation's future that we were unable to see the gifts already present in our congregational life—we didn't see the centering prayer group, the vibrant choir, the talented potters, painters, and dancers. And we missed the gifts in our neighborhood. When we talked about our low-income neighbors immediately around the building, we always saw them as needy people rather than as gifted people—frankly, the way we were seeing the newer, more affluent neighbors to our south.

We in the congregation were missing the vibrant children who spilled around the chancel at the Children's Moment time in worship. We were missing the talents that artists in the neighborhood were bringing, designing T-shirts celebrating their neighbors with wit and love. We were missing the life around us and within us because we weren't looking at what gifts we already held in our hands.

Coming Face to Face with "Parradoux"

As the summer of 2003 headed toward fall, I heard from De'Amon Harges, a friend I had made in South Bend. When I met De'Amon in 2000, he was an artist and called himself "Parradoux." Twenty-six years old, African-American, with dreadlocks, a shining smile, and a wrestler's build, he knew how to command a room. He worked at the drug and alcohol rehab center up the street from the church. People he worked with had told him he should talk with me when I returned from my sabbatical. And people I worked with had told me I should talk with this artist who worked up the street. When we finally met, I asked him to tell me a story. Asking for a story is a common practice of mine when I first meet someone, because it often reveals surprising truths that the usual practiced pleasantries hide.

He told me about his grandfather, a life-long resident of South Bend. As a young man, his grandfather and his family had lived by "the lake" (a toxic dump site) in the projects on the west side of South Bend, a segregated area. His grandfather had been a singer on the "chitlin' circuit." (During the days of legal segregation, those were venues where black artists were allowed to perform.) His grandfather had planted a tree they called "the Learning Tree" in the projects. De'Amon explained how his grandfather would gather people around it, talking with the young people and giving other elders a chance to tell stories, particularly in times of tension and drama.

> We were missing the talents that artists in the neighborhood were bringing, designing T-shirts celebrating their neighbors with wit and love. We were missing the life around us and within us because we weren't looking at what gifts we already held in our hands.

De'Amon had inherited his grandfather's magic touch with young people. He started hanging around the church building in South Bend and met some of the young people who lived nearby. One of them was a tall, white teenager who used to skateboard in our neighborhood, his blond hair flapping around his head. He and a group of his friends started hanging out with De'Amon.

They were also artists—graffiti artists. When I asked De'Amon to paint the fading playground equipment at the church, he asked if he could hire these teenagers to join him in the effort. It was a great idea. The project had the possibility of turning these teens from enemies who were vandalizing the church into friends who were making it more beautiful!

In 2001 De'Amon left South Bend for Chicago, and in 2003, by way of a job transfer, he moved to Indianapolis shortly after I did. This is when he and I reconnected, and soon he started walking the four blocks from his home to Broadway to see me several times a week. He always brought a story about someone he met along the walk.

He told me about the man who sat on his porch playing chess and how young people gathered around and talked with him and challenged him to a game. He told me about the young men who stood on street corners, talking and keeping an eye on things in the neighborhood. He learned who the artists were, and who the teachers were, and who the entrepreneurs were.

De'Amon began walking the four blocks from his
home to Broadway to see me several times a week.
He always brought a story about someone he met
along the walk.

He told me about the man who sat on his porch
playing chess and how young people gathered
around and talked with him and challenged him
to a game. He told me about the young men who
stood on street corners, talking and keeping an eye
on things in the neighborhood. He learned who the
artists were, and who the teachers were, and who
the entrepreneurs were.

At Broadway we held church meetings almost every night.
De'Amon asked if he could drop by then with a different neighbor
each time and introduce him or her at the meeting. He knew that
if people just met each other as neighbors, it would change their
relationship. Of course I said yes.

So De'Amon would drop by at the beginning of the meeting. "Oh, hi, everybody—sorry to interrupt. My friend Kwanzaa
and I were just stopping by the church. I'm showing him around.
He lives up the street and leads the Indianapolis Reggae Band.
Would y'all mind meeting him and introducing yourself to him?"
De'Amon was quick to mention a particular gift or interest that was
part of the neighbor's life. It was brilliant. Church members (most
of whom didn't live near the church) were beginning to meet the
church's neighbors, not as recipients of the church's charity but
simply as the people who lived nearby.

I had often found myself thinking, "I wish I knew how to bring
these different groups of people together in meaningful ways." But

maybe *I* didn't have to know how—maybe I could support those who did. People like my friend De'Amon. One of the paradoxes I was learning was that I didn't have to be the lead actor in order to help. Others were much better positioned to do that good work. I could just give it an assist.

The Roving Listener

Inside the church, we were beginning to notice the giftedness of the people we had formerly seen as recipients of our services, and changes were happening in the neighborhoods surrounding ours. In 2005 the neighborhood development corporation was preparing to put together a strategic plan. They contacted the church and asked us to "partner" with them. We knew it meant they wanted money to help pay for pulling the plan together. We also knew that strategic plans, almost inevitably, begin with a needs survey.

Our leaders went back to the organization and said, "We'll partner with you on this task, but only if you do it by building a plan based on the gifts, not the needs, of our neighbors." They agreed. We added, "Since we're putting up half the money, you need to let us pick the person to lead this survey, and we'll supervise the person we select." Again they agreed.

De'Amon was already doing this work, so we asked him if he wanted to do it formally and get paid for it. He was thrilled. We called the position "The Roving Listener," and De'Amon began by taking a different block every week and visiting every household on that block. He talked with every person of every age in every house. After he finished his survey of a block, he gathered together all of its residents and also invited people from the development corporation and the church to attend the gathering. He asked the corporation and church representatives not to speak except to ask clarifying questions. Their job was to listen and learn about the gifts of their neighbors.

At the first of these meetings, a man in his thirties brought his portfolio. He worked for a hip-hop magazine and showed off some of his work. He was also a photographer. The woman whose home we were meeting in baked a beautiful and delicious chocolate cake. (We later hired her to provide baked goods for events at the church.) Another neighbor said he wanted to do a neighborhood clean-up. Another mentioned a neighbor who wasn't present at the meeting ("he doesn't like things like this"), but he was sure he could get him to help in the clean-up. His enthusiastic offer was instructive for the corporation and church leaders present. For years the church had organized just such an event. This man and his neighbor lived half-a-block away from the church and had never participated in it—didn't even seem aware of it, in fact. What a revelation that was! And each of the subsequent gatherings revealed untapped treasures in the lives of more of our neighbors.

When De'Amon began his work, he discovered something pretty quickly. Before starting the job, he had knocked on doors as a neighbor, and people had talked with him easily, welcoming him into their homes. But when he began this new job by introducing himself as a representative of the church and the development corporation, people weren't very welcoming to him. So he went back to what worked. He told me that people didn't trust institutions, but they trusted neighbors.

Every week De'Amon e-mailed a report to the development corporation and the church. He shared what he had learned by visiting people's homes—things people don't think to tell you, things so much a part of their lives they don't consider them distinctive. He learned these things by paying attention to the awards on the walls, the food he could smell cooking, and the music he heard playing in the rooms.

De'Amon was learning other things from these visits, too. He realized that he shouldn't directly ask people what their gifts were—when he did, people hemmed and hawed, and when he did get an answer, he wasn't always sure it was accurate. He didn't think people were lying; it was just that they weren't used to talking about themselves. So, he began to ask other people what they thought of their neighbors, their housemates, their family members. And when De'Amon mentioned the skills he had heard about to the people who had them—slyly bringing up making cakes to a woman he'd learned was a gifted baker, or mentioning singing to the man he'd learned had a rare tenor—they almost always bubbled over with excitement about it.

In this process De'Amon also learned the difference between an opinion and an idea that will make a person get up off the couch and act (what social theorist Paulo Freire called "generative themes"). One day De'Amon said to me, "Mike, you have an opinion about nearly everything. But you'll only do something about a few things. What are the things you care enough about to actually do?" That made perfect sense to me. I play the trumpet. I read. I take walks. All of those things are commitments of mine, not because anyone has asked me to do them, but simply because I care about them. That question made De'Amon and me start wondering how the church could find out about those things our neighbors already do.

I remembered that when I would talk with neighbors back in the 1980s and early 1990s, it was often to find out what they thought should be happening around the neighborhood. They suggested the church run a recreation program focused on the older boys, or start a child care center for the younger kids, or an employment program for the older ones. In those years I never thought to notice what they were already immersed in and committed to in their own lives or ask about what positive things they were doing.

When I finally started paying attention, I saw that Ernie, one of the many mothers of young children who lived on the church block, was someone who everyone would go to in a crisis. She always seemed to know what to say when people were hurting, or grieving, or angry. She could bind a physical wound or comfort another parent who was frustrated with his own child.

Why hadn't I noticed that before?

I met teenagers who designed their own T-shirts and then sold them to others around the neighborhood. This wasn't an underground market, but it wasn't on my radar. Again, I hadn't been paying attention to what my neighbors were already doing.

The lesson I learned from De'Amon was tearing the scales from my eyes. I could see the cooks, entrepreneurs, artists, and organizers all at work with one another. I still didn't have many practices that helped me know what to do with the gifts and passions once I saw them—but seeing was a good first practice. Seeing gave me the opportunity to experiment by inviting people to share their gift or passion with others in the neighborhood and around the congregation.

De'Amon's lesson reinforced the idea of focusing our efforts on building on what is present rather than what is not. No wonder our old summer program didn't change the odds for everyone! We hadn't been focused on what people cared about and had to offer one another.

As De'Amon's visits increased, the buzz around the neighborhood grew. Some people would phone their neighbors to ask if they knew what De'Amon was up to and whether he was legitimate or not. Some neighbors met him openly, eager to tell their stories. Others wanted to know what was going to happen with the information they shared.

In the congregation, the church leadership (lay and clergy) began to invite people to share their gifts with us. We had a neighborhood masseuse set up her table out on the front lawn of the church and offer massages as people left worship. Parishioners bought jewelry from a woman who also gave them manicures. We hired neighborhood cooks to host meals in their homes or to cook for events at the church.

Around this time, a local university put an intern from the school of social work in our parish. She met many of the artists that De'Amon had identified through his work, and she organized an arts festival over a three-day weekend, with neighborhood artists displaying their pieces and selling them. A woodworker in a wheelchair who lived in a basement apartment several blocks from the church showed off his carvings, checkers sets, and walking sticks. Another artist shared the furniture he made, alongside paintings and pottery he created. One young man created images from broken pieces of LPs: one was of Bob Marley and another was of the Beatles' iconic *Abbey Road* album cover. A grandmother raising her two grandsons displayed her sewing and crafts.

The development corporation just didn't know what to do with the revelation of these abundant gifts. They were so used to building a strategic plan based on the needs of the neighborhood that they couldn't figure out how to build a plan focused on the gifts of the neighbors. Even though De'Amon put together a report about these gifts and gave it to the corporation, they filed the report away and eventually lost it.

Despite the development corporation's failure to understand, De'Amon cultivated the gifts he was seeing. At his request, a neighbor hosted a group of neighborhood artists at her home. There was a lot of energy in the room that night. All of the artists brought examples of their work, and they talked and occasionally argued long into that night about the meaning of their work and how to get it shared in the larger world. De'Amon also arranged gatherings of gardeners and adults who cared deeply about young people. Entrepreneurs got together, and so did musicians.

De'Amon's work broadened our view of our neighbors dramatically. And it also caused us to re-think the programming we had been delivering to our neighbors. We had been tinkering with the summer program since 2003, continuing to structure our offerings around classes for young people. The problem wasn't the people; it was the assumptions from within the church that the young people didn't have something to offer, that they needed to be fixed and corrected. The program had aimed at teaching people what they don't know rather than building on what they do know.

How Do We Gather Abundance?

In March 2008, I felt something needed to change. The previous December, we had applied for funding for the 2008 summer program, saying we were going to run the same program we had been running for nearly twenty years. But thanks to De'Amon's work, we were seeing the gifts around us more and more clearly. What would the summer program look like if we applied De'Amon's insights to it?

Calling together the summer program leaders (church members and staff), I told them we weren't going to do the summer program anymore. "What are we going to do then?" they asked. I said (honestly), "I don't know. Let's take a couple of days to pray about it and think it over. The only thing I know is we won't work with 25 kids, or 50 kids, or 150 kids anymore. What we do will involve everybody who lives in our corner of the neighborhood. That's about 4,000 people. And none of it will involve registration forms."

If we were going to make a difference that changed the odds for everybody, we needed to have everybody in mind as we shaped what would come next. We prayed together, and over the next few days we caught one another in the hallways and streets and talked. Ideas were taking shape around how to gather the abundance in our community.

Over the next few months, we created a new summer experience we called "Name, Bless, and Connect." The governing council and church staff committed to hire young people from the neighborhood around us (and a few adults) to name the gifts, talents, dreams, and passions they saw in the lives of their neighbors, lay hands on them and bless them, and connect them to other people (both near and far) who cared about the same thing. We would build on the work De'Amon had been doing.

The summer staff (two women from our neighborhood who had run the old summer program, and the pastor for youth, children, and families at Broadway) gamely put our plans into place.

They took the church's old thrift shop and converted it into "The Loaves and Fishes Room." They bought large, brightly colored Post-it Notes—both the familiar squares and the ones shaped like arrows. After the young people visited folks in the neighborhood, they brought back the names and gifts of the people they met. For each gift in the life of someone they visited, they created a Post-it Note and put it on the wall. After just one week, the walls were beginning to fill up with names. The leaders gathered with the young rovers in front of the walls of Post-it Notes and mixed and matched people and their gifts. They used the arrows to literally connect the names of the people on the walls and talked about how to take that connection off the walls and into the streets.

The young rovers were discovering the richness around them. One day they met a man who had created "The Dirty Dozen Hunting and Fishing Club." When they asked him why he did that, he told them that when he was a child, Fall Creek had been the place where he learned about life. The men there had showed him how to bait a hook, how to develop the patience to wait until the fish was caught, and how to carefully remove the hook from the fish's mouth. They'd taught him how to play sports, and they'd taught him respect for nature and for other people. Every day after school he would go down to Fall Creek and watch as the men in the neighborhood fished in those waters. "That was my school," he told the young people. He was grateful for what those men taught him and for the waters that fed him, his family, and his community. He told the young people, "I talk to the creek and the creek talks to me, and I tell it I will not forsake it."

The young people also met women who were poets and seamstresses. They met men who were musicians and artists. They met women who ran businesses and who fished. They met men who cooked and gardened. They were both showing the parish and seeing for themselves that in this neighborhood, our cup runneth over!

What happened next? Very slowly we experimented with what the young people were finding. Many of them struck up friendships with neighbors they hadn't met before. One young man who loved working on cars discovered an older neighbor who loved the same thing, and they spent hours together tinkering under the hood of a car and talking about cars and life. Later that summer they were invited to a meal at the home of a church member whose son works on and repairs airline engines. They spent the evening together talking about the way different engines work and the varieties of places one can work on cars, trucks, and airplanes.

Another young man working in the summer program met a couple who had recently moved into the neighborhood and who were alumni of his high school. The neighbors invited him into their home to show him the wall dedicated to their shared high school—the wall on which they had no fewer than twenty pictures of high school classmates and alumni gatherings, as well as newspaper headlines that featured their school. As they talked together, the couple asked the young man how he was doing in his classes. When he told them about his high GPA, they asked him why he was so successful. He told them that the killing of his brother a year and a half before had caused him to raise his commitment to work hard on his education and avoid his brother's fate. He had rarely spoken of his brother's death, but now he had built a deep connection with his new neighbors, who would serve as a safe harbor when he was struggling with the challenges of his life.

Because of developments like these, the neighbors began to see the young people not as troublesome teens, but as valuable connectors who made their community stronger. One day our young rovers were stopped by a neighbor who brought his twelve-year-old son out to meet them. The father told the young people about his son's gifts. To illustrate, he brought out an armful of his son's student awards for a variety of activities. The father told the young people, "I know you're good people, because I hear about the work you're doing. How can my son join you?"

As people's desires to be seen and to celebrate one another's gifts became increasingly clear to the church staff and lay leadership, we listened and watched what was happening. We paid attention to where the Holy Spirit was active, where the energy was in the conversations. We watched people's body language. We asked follow-up questions. And then when we saw people acting, we asked if we could be a part of what they were doing.

The need to move away from trying to help or fix people is more than a practical problem. It's a spiritual problem, too. When I had lived in South Bend years before, an interfaith council asked me to be part of a panel that tackled the question "What is the biggest spiritual problem in South Bend?" When it was my turn to speak, all I said was this: "The biggest spiritual problem in South Bend is that the poor don't believe they have any gifts, and the rich don't believe they have any needs." The same could be said for Indianapolis.

Another aspect of the problem was the communication, or lack thereof, among different groups of people. Seana, for example, was very aware of her giftedness. So was Adele. Yet even gifted, passionate women like these believed that what they offered wasn't valued by anyone: the police officers who found them suspicious, the school teachers and administrators who saw them as uninvolved parents, the social workers who seemed to change the rules on them every day, and the clergy and laity in religious institutions who viewed them as sinners separate from themselves.

As I learned about the many ways that police and clergy communicated their disregard to Seana, Adele, and my other neighbors, I began to notice the subtle and not-so-subtle ways that Christian congregational life tended to focus on people's needs rather than their capacities. The prayers and hymns and choral anthems often depict the poor, homeless, and sick only by what they lack. In the hymn "Together We Serve," we are "extending [God's] love to the last and the least" as if the "last and the least" don't have something to teach the rest of us about extending God's love. Where is the hymn that celebrates the abundance of talent and gift that overflows every neighborhood? Where are the sermons that invite us to see the less fortunate as agents of God's healing rather than encourage us to act on behalf of the less fortunate? Where are the prayers that not only ask God to give the hungry good things, but also give thanks for the good things God has already so lavishly given them?

Just Because You Have Sight

In her book *Wise Blood,* Flannery O'Connor introduces a preacher named Hazel Motes. Hazel proclaims, "I preach the Church Without Christ. I'm member and preacher to that church where the blind don't see and the lame don't walk and what's dead stays that way." Through Hazel, O'Connor offers her critique of the church. The church is often blind to the change we say God in Christ has brought into the world.

Rev. Rachel, my co-pastor, met with a group of young people who are biologically blind. "How does the seeing world treat you?" she asked.

"That's not the right language. It's the 'sighted' world, not the 'seeing' world," one of them said to her. "Just because you have sight doesn't mean you can see."

A leader of our congregation is blind. If we treated him as if he could not see, we would miss some of the wisest leadership in the church. He is blind, but he *sees.*

The blindness of the sighted is the way of the world. Unfortunately, it is also often the way of the church and other religious communities.

And yet, the world is also graced with people who understand, and are curious about, the abundance in the world all around us. I've found that some of my deepest learning has come at the feet of experts in "secular" disciplines. People from our parish have visited with economists, physicians, writers, artists, and teachers who specialize in ferreting out hard-to-see abundance.

In 2010, a few folks from our church traveled to Philadelphia to visit physician John Rich, an African-American who grew up in the Bronx. As a medical student at Harvard Medical School, he refused to work at Massachusetts General Hospital. He wanted, he said, to work with people "who look like me." He went to work at one of the hospitals mainly serving the poor in Boston. Young men came in who had been shot and stabbed, young men who looked like him. When they recovered, he hired some of them to serve as health advocates for what he called the Health Crew. He asked, "Who knows more about health in their communities, and who cares more about health in their communities?" This was a powerful question for me and my church community to hear. It was a question I had never asked anyone before, nor had I ever been asked this question: "Who are the healers in your community?"

The question he quickly asked on the heels of the first was simple yet powerful: "What are you doing to support them?"

Today, when you set foot inside Broadway Church in Indianapolis, you will see signs that ask "Who are the healers?" and "Who are the teachers?" and "Who are the artists?" On one wall in the building, these signs hang next to mirrors, so that we can see and remember that *we* are the healers, the teachers, and the artists.

Making the Invisible Visible

When Adele came to us, we asked her to tell us about her gifts. That's one reason we could see that she was a magnificent cook: we asked.

When De'Amon interrupted church meetings to introduce people from the neighborhood, people from the congregation began seeing past all the labels they had applied to this group. When the young people in the summer program began to talk with their neighbors and pay attention to their neighbors' gifts, they began

> Now, more than developing great church pro-
> gramming, we were developing new patterns of
> church, new ways of being neighbor. We were
> trying to see what was right in front of us, hidden
> in plain sight.

meeting gardeners and cooks, artists and poets, business women
and men—so many gifted people it was hard to keep up.

For decades, the young people in our neighborhood had been
bussed out to a school system over half an hour away, to a white
suburban world that told them they were unwanted and lived in a
bad neighborhood and had bad parents and neighbors who didn't
care. Now they were seeing what they knew to be true: abundance
encountered in every corner of their lives.

Now, more than developing great church programming, we
were developing new patterns of church, new ways of being neighbor. We were trying to see what was right in front of us, hidden in
plain sight.

3

Noticing People's Gifts

Once we see people's gifts, how are we going to build on what we see? How can we make it clear to others that those who are often thought of as empty can be recognized as people overflowing with gifts?

In Acts 3, Peter and John walk up the steps of the temple and encounter a man who is lame. Faithful friends have carried him there every day so that he can beg for alms. When he asks Peter and John for money, they reply, "Silver and gold have we none, but we offer you all that we have. In the name of Jesus Christ, get up and walk." And immediately, the man is "walking and leaping and praising God."

I wanted to experience the joy of that moment. When people stopped by the church asking for emergency assistance and I wrote checks to fix the problem, they never left my office leaping with joy. Somehow through the years I had rewritten the story to say, "Silver and gold have we some. Here you go. See you later." I wanted the men and women who received our church's aid to leap with joy, and I wanted to leap, too. But the truth is that our Christian practice and that of social service agencies in this country and abroad aren't very similar to this story of giving in Acts. They're a lot more like our food pantry, circa 1992—focused only on the needs and not interested in celebrating the healing and joy in people's lives.

I wasn't able to tap into the joy because, when the church door opened and a stranger walked in, I went into problem-solving mode. I thought the problem was that people needed food. But I didn't know most of the people who came through the doors. I hadn't been inside many of their homes and learned who they were. I wasn't *seeing* the people before me. Instead, I was seeing a stereotype: poor people who needed the help of the church. And I thought a bag of groceries was the best we could do. People walked away, grateful for the food, but with their spirits and heads down.

One of the realities in low-income inner-city neighborhoods is that life and its struggles aren't hidden. If there are problems, everyone knows about them. When young men are arrested or die in the streets, when women feed their drug addiction by selling their bodies in prostitution, it's not possible to pretend everything is all right.

What I hadn't been seeing were the gifts present in the midst of the crises. When I realized this, I knew our church had to change. We began asking ourselves how to make the gifts as visible and widely known as the struggles. And we began asking ourselves how our church could embolden—rather than merely supplement or, worse, replace—the good things that were already happening around us.

The School of the Spirit

When my family and I moved back to South Bend, our older son began kindergarten. I went to sign him up at the elementary school, and I filled out a long form asking, among other things, if I was willing to volunteer in the school office. They said they were looking for some volunteers with computer skills, and I told them I had those. But no one called, and that felt lousy. Did the school not call because they didn't think I could be helpful? Or were they so disorganized that they weren't following up with anyone?

In our food pantry survey, we asked people, "What are you good enough at that you could teach someone else how to do it?" We asked, but a year later, much like the staff at my son's school, I hadn't called and followed up with people. It took a conversation I had with Joe, a folk musician, painter, and electrical engineer who was unemployed, to make something happen. Joe asked if he could offer some music classes at the church—he wanted to teach neighborhood kids to play the guitar and the keyboard. Imagining Joe teaching chords and scales to Destiny and Andrae inspired me to think that maybe the people who filled out our survey would want to teach, too.

And so we started "The School of the Spirit." Many of the visitors to our food pantry were the school's teachers. Anyone who could find at least three students could offer a class in anything: cooking, car repair, song-writing. The church wasn't going to find the students for them; that was each teacher's responsibility. But when they had at least three students, we'd provide any needed materials: the ingredients for a cooking class, air filters for a car repair class, paints and canvas and brushes for an art class, and so on. We placed a coffee can in each room, and if the students put any money in it, the teacher got to keep it.

There were classes in music, painting, Tai Chi, conversational physics, film, Mexican cooking, basic auto repair, and quilt-making. We held several rounds of these classes over several years. New classes were added; some of the old ones dropped off.

In the third year, we began to offer a six-week "semester" in what we called Broadway University (or "old B.U."). We took the most successful courses—Mexican Cooking, Conversational Physics, and The History of the Hollywood Western and Why Black Men Were Left Out—and charged students tuition up front.

When the local newspaper ran a small story on the school, we got a call from a woman who was interested in taking the class on "conversational psychics." I told her, "I'm sorry, but it's a class on conversational *physics*."

"Oh," she said, "then I'm not interested at all." (Later I wondered what a class on conversational psychics would be like. I supposed it would be very quiet, as they would all know what each other was thinking.)

I began to feel some of that leaping with joy described in Acts, and I think the teachers and students did, too. Yes, the church still ran the food pantry. But the most important thing we provided was an opportunity for all of us to learn from one another. Everyone had something to teach. And many people wanted to teach (and earn a little income in the process). The food pantry had been a place where food was dispensed and people were sent away; now it became a way to find out what gifts people had to share. We could invest in those persons and their gifts and let others know about them. The people once known as food pantry recipients were now known as teachers who knew something people wanted to learn.

What the World Considers Trash

In October of 1992, two blocks from the church in South Bend, a seven-year-old named Columbus Coleman was shot and killed in the middle of the afternoon while playing in his grandmother's front yard. He was an innocent victim. As two men were chasing each other in his neighborhood, they shot at each other, they missed, and one of them hit the little boy. There was a neighborhood meeting at the church the next night. The place was packed, and the emotions expressed were raw and powerful: grief, anger, hope, despair, comfort.

After the meeting, the parents of a fourteen-year-old boy named Aaron talked with a church member; the parents said they were worried about keeping their son out of trouble during the coming summer. They both worked, and they couldn't figure out how to keep him busy while they were gone.

The outreach committee met and decided to give Aaron a job. We didn't have the money to do it, but we did have more than six months to raise the money. What was the job going to be? We wanted to put him to work sharing his gifts in the neighborhood. The committee recognized how unwise it would be to just hire a fourteen-year-old boy and turn him loose, so they decided to hire a recent college graduate, John, to work with him. John had grown up in a Midwest inner city, and I knew he wouldn't be intimidated by our neighborhood.

We called John our first "Animator of the Spirit." His entire job description was "to pull out the talents of Aaron for the benefit of the larger community." The outreach committee asked Aaron's family to house the Animator of the Spirit for the summer and gave them a small stipend to cover the cost of feeding him.

It was important for John to live with Aaron's family so he could say to Aaron, "Look how much your parents appreciate your good work," and so he could say to Aaron's parents, "Look what good work your son is doing in the community." It was important for him to say these things because those of us who knew this family were aware they were having problems communicating with one another in kind ways. When John offered these concrete words of celebration, he was reminding Aaron and his parents of the joy and care they had for one another. The outreach committee had a hunch this would produce fertile soil in which Aaron's gifts could blossom.

The committee was right. Shortly after John began his job, Aaron took him on a walk around the neighborhood, and they talked about things Aaron loved, like computers and art. Aaron took John to the Boys and Girls Club, where they discovered computers under a tarp in a corner of the club. The director said they didn't work, and John asked Aaron to try to repair them. After Aaron got several of them working, John asked the director if

Aaron could teach a class on how to use the computer to any of the kids who came in. She said "Yes," and Aaron taught a class to his younger neighbors.

With the endorsement of the church's trustees, John asked Aaron to teach an art class at the church. In the class, Aaron asked the children, his neighbors, to draw pictures of the neighborhood. Since the killing of the little boy the previous fall, the images of their neighborhood that appeared in the newspaper and on television were terrible. There were photos of trash and even some needles scattered among playground equipment at the park. There were videos on the news of young men being arrested and of women working as prostitutes on the street.

So what the children drew surprised me at first. They drew a boat on the river that ran through the neighborhood. They drew people singing in the neighborhood park. They drew trees and flowers. They drew buildings and a fancy car driving through their streets. They knew the reality that was shown through the media, but that wasn't where their eyes went first. They thought of the good things about their place, their home. And like John's praise of Aaron's work and Aaron's parents' appreciation, it served to remind the young people and their families of the goodness and joy that were present in their community.

Soon about fifty children were hanging out with Aaron and the Animator. They decided to do a neighborhood clean-up, and in the process they collected over a hundred pounds of broken glass (a staple of urban communities). What should they do with it? The kids wanted money for it, but the recycler only offered them five dollars. That didn't seem like enough to them, so they turned to John and Aaron for some ideas.

At the local high school, Aaron and John talked with the art teacher, who was working during the summer. He suggested they make a mosaic with the broken glass. Aaron asked John (who was an artist as well) how to do that, and together they worked out a plan.

What the children drew surprised me at first. They drew a boat on the river that ran through the neighborhood. They drew people singing in the neighborhood park. They drew trees and flowers. They drew buildings and a fancy car driving through their streets. They knew the reality that was shown through the media, but that wasn't where their eyes went first. They thought of the good things about their place, their home. It served to remind the young people and their families of the goodness and joy that were present in their community.

They divided the fifty young people into three groups, two groups of seventeen and one group of sixteen. Then they took a piece of plywood that measured eight feet by four feet and divided it into thirds. Next they took the kids' drawings from the art class and sketched them out on the plywood. And then, working in three shifts, they created the mosaic. Some of the glass they spray-painted a variety of colors. Other pieces they left in their natural green, blue, clear, and brown. The mosaic included all the images they'd created in Aaron's class and two others. One was a rendering of Mr. Groves's candy store, a tiny building just large enough to hold one adult and one child, and the other picture was the largest building in downtown, a multi-storied bank building. But when they put these in the mosaic, Mr. Groves's candy store was bigger than the bank building!

As our church looked at the mosaic, it became the symbol of seeing and celebrating the abundance in our world. In large letters on the right side, the mosaic proclaimed "You are the light of the world." The same neighborhood presented in the newspapers as "bad" was seen through the eyes of the children as a place full of life and joy, singing and water, colors and nature.

That piece of art, made from broken glass swept up from the inner-city streets, now hangs on the front wall of the sanctuary in South Bend. What the world considered trash is great art decorating the walls of an important building.

Art was opening my eyes and the eyes of others. The only subject I ever failed in my academic career was sixth-grade art class. But I was coming to understand that the work of ministry and the work of community is more of an art—a matter of seeing differently and then acting on that seeing—than a science.

In the first chapter I mentioned a group of young people who were covering the church in South Bend with graffiti. With the church's support, De'Amon hired them to paint the playground equipment, and as they were doing that, the curator of the regional museum of art was visiting and saw their work. I knew that he often came by our church building on certain days, and I made sure the young people were working then, so he could see and appreciate these young artists. And he was impressed: he hired them to be part of an exhibit on the Holocaust he was curating.

We were discovering gifts, but in really unexpected places. Often we found them arising out of the ashes of tragedy, pain, violence, and grief. Painting, drawing, dancing, movement, poetry, and music revealed truth that I was missing in more routine church practices.

Everyone Wants to Give

Learning to pay attention to the gifts around us was a slow, unfolding process. I was still having difficulty breaking the habit of listening to discern people's needs. But sometimes the gift presented itself so clearly in those conversations that even I couldn't miss it.

I often thought of the young black men in our neighborhood as part of the problem. Many of them weren't going to school. Some were perpetrators of the violence around us. To me they seemed threatening and aggressive. But I realize now that what I saw when I looked at them were the caricatures I had created. I saw uneducated, sullen young men whom my parishioners tried to avoid everywhere—in the street, in stores, in schools.

Still, I knew many of these young men well enough to have regular conversations with them. Early on, they would curse me out or pointedly ignore me, but that didn't last. I made it clear that I wasn't going away. I would sit and listen to their stories, and they could tell I was trying to learn who they were. I was present. They tried to educate me about KRS-One, Boogie Down Productions, and Public Enemy—the music they listened to that spoke the truth they saw around them, and the dreams they had for themselves and for their families.

Standing in the parking lot one day in late fall, I overheard "Fat Mike," a neighborhood teenager (who wasn't overweight), saying, "The church doesn't do anything around this community." I challenged him to talk with me about it. He agreed, but because he wanted to see if I was really serious about having the conversation, he set the meeting for one in the morning at a local restaurant.

At about 1:10 at the Waffle House, I clutched my hot chocolate and asked Mike to make a reasonable suggestion about something the church could do "for the community" and told him we would try to do it. What did he have in mind? Mike first offered the idea of the church paying a utility bill for everyone on his block. I laughed out loud. I knew his gas bill was over $500, and we couldn't pay it for him, much less every other neighbor on the block. He threw out a few more suggestions that were similarly problematic, and then he offered something from his heart. "Me and my friends could dress up like Santa Claus and go door-to-door on our block on Christmas Eve."

I was stunned. "Sure," I said. "So what can the church do?"

"Can you get us the Santa Claus suits?"

"Of course," I said. "What else?" I pulled out a pad of paper and took notes as he laid out the plan.

"We'll get together on Christmas Eve. After dark. That's the best time. We'll go door-to-door and bring along candy and presents. People will be really surprised!"

As we moved closer to Christmas, Mike and his friends worked the plan he had put together. They went to Frog's Records and Tapes around the corner and bought cassette singles (it was the eighties) and candy. They gift-wrapped the cassettes and candy in Christmas paper. They tried on Santa suits at the local costume shop. When Seana, back home on the block after her first year in college, heard what they were doing, she put together a little scrapbook for each home on the block. Every scrapbook contained memories of life on the block and an individual poem for each family, penned by Seana.

Christmas Eve arrived, and so did the Santa suits. After dark, the young men put on the suits and started down their block. Seana followed along with a camera. I walked with them, but stayed on the periphery, not wanting to put myself in the center of the Santas' activity. This was Mike's idea, and he and his friends had done the work. I was just the investor.

No one on the block was expecting these visitors. At the first house I worried that the appearance of three Santa Clauses would be confusing to the children. I was wrong. They received them as kings! I heard the cries of joy erupting from inside the home. Laughter and hand slaps and hugs all around. After Seana took a group shot, they passed out the family's gifts. Then it was on to the next house. As the joyous procession moved down the street, it grew larger as several people from the homes already visited joined the parade. At the last house, the raucous, loving crowd barely fit into the living room.

Everyone wants to give. Everyone. Even young African-American men who are often labeled as troublemakers, addicts,

> Everyone wants to give. Everyone. Even young
> African-American men who are often labeled as
> troublemakers, addicts, gang members, or at-risk
> teens. These young men wanted to make a contri-
> bution to the place and people they called home.

gang members, or at-risk teens. These young men wanted to make a contribution to the place and people they called home. They hadn't wanted to get something from Santa Claus; they wanted to *be* Santa Claus! Broadway's contribution was small. Theirs was large. And their neighbors knew it, saw it, and celebrated it with them. Something was being born that night. Something right before our eyes. On the night the church was celebrating the birth of Christ, our neighbors were coming to see the annoying teenagers on their block as the gift givers!

Why, I asked myself later, was it so hard for me and for our congregation, and even for the neighbors, to see these young men as something other than a problem?

I was trying to unpack this issue with a man who was both a Pentecostal minister and the junk man on the block. I told him that while I could see the young men's eagerness to add delight to the lives of their neighbors, I didn't know how to further invest in their giftedness. I had tools (whether effective or ineffective) to fix people, not help them shine. Even the prayers offered in the sanctuary on Sunday mornings were focusing on the problem and brokenness of these young men, not blessing the gifts they showed in their lives. Some part of me knew I needed to abandon the script that told me I was there to fix other men's brokenness. But I just didn't know how to set that script down or what to replace it with.

My conversation partner interrupted me as I poured out my confusion. "We're always putting the cart of material issues before the horse of the Spirit," he said. At first I didn't understand what he meant, but his colorful reframing of a familiar expression stayed with me. I was seeing these young men as people with material problems—lack of training, or education, or socialization—and I was missing the spiritual giftedness that lay in the hearts and lives of each of them.

The Major Taylor Bicycle Recycling Center and School

I was to learn this lesson over and over again. I'm still learning it today. Often conversations in the pews on Sunday morning have led me to new lessons, new teachers.

One Sunday a neighborhood woman showed up for worship, then sat in the pew afterwards, weeping. When I asked her what was the matter, she told me that her son was about to get kicked out of school. She asked me to talk with him.

I stopped by her home on a Tuesday night. Donna was sitting in a chair. Across from her, lying on the couch, was her son, Adrian, watching television. As soon as I came in, she started crying about how much trouble he was in and saying he was no good.

I turned to her son and said, "At our church we believe that every person has something to offer, and we believe it's a sin to waste it. Is there anything that you do well enough that you could teach someone else how to do it?"

He was still watching television, lying flat on his back. He didn't look at me as he said, "I play football."

At this his mother stopped crying and became very animated. "Oh, yeah," she said. "Before he got in all this trouble, he was playing both ways—offense and defense. The coaches love him."

At that point Adrian sat up. The television was still on, but some of his attention was on me. "Do you think you know how to teach younger kids how to play football?"

He said yes, and then wove stories about blocking drills, and linebacker hits, and how to keep someone from fumbling.

I said, "That's not a bad idea. But it's February in South Bend right now, not a great time to be outdoors playing football. Is there anything else you could teach people?"

"I fix things. If the remote control breaks, I fix it," he said as he played with it in his hands.

I thought, *Wow! I've got nineteen years of education, and if my remote control breaks, I go buy a new one.*

"Can you fix anything else?" I asked.

"Well," Adrian said, "me and my neighbor, we fix bikes." I asked him how the brakes and the gears work, and he told me in enough detail that I knew he could do it.

"I have a friend who likes to repair bikes," I said. "Do you think you and your friend are interested in joining forces with my friend and doing something about it?"

He said yes, and the next day I came by his house with my friend. Adrian and his friend were there, and I prayed with all of them: "Gracious God, bless these three as they share their love and knowledge of bicycles with neighbors near and far. . . ." Over the next couple of months, they started what they came to call the Major Taylor Bicycle Recycling Center and School in an unused garage at a church member's home in the neighborhood. (In the early 1900s, Major Taylor was an African-American world-class cyclist from Indiana.)

Adrian and the others would get together every day after school and on Saturday mornings to work in the garage. The first couple of weeks, they were busy turning the garage into a shop with workbenches, a place for their tools, and even a few chairs, so that if neighbors, young or old, stopped by, they could sit and visit while Adrian and company worked. With a grant they received from the St. Joseph County Community Foundation, they bought three sets of tools, bike helmets, and seats.

My friend had connections at Notre Dame (he was getting a Ph.D. in international relations there), and they got several bikes donated from the end-of-the-year sale at the school. They cleaned the bikes up, repaired the ones that needed it, and then sold them. The first bicycles they repaired for a customer were for a Notre Dame professor, and they got two pizzas and three cases of pop in exchange for the work. When the shop first opened, they negotiated the cost of the repair with the bike owner before starting the work. After a few months they developed a fee structure, but they would occasionally repair someone's bicycle for free if they knew the cyclist and knew the person couldn't afford the repair. As the word spread, people would often give the shop bicycles in various states of repair or disrepair. Some of them Adrian and his coworkers sold, and some of them they salvaged for parts that they used in their repairs or sold to customers who needed a pedal or a kickstand or a seat.

On Saturdays, Adrian and Co. invited kids from the neighborhood to come to the shop. They'd teach a brief bicycle safety class, give an exam, and then reward the participants with new bicycle helmets that an elderly couple in the neighborhood had bought for them to share with children.

When I went to Adrian's house that first night, I didn't do much. But the little I did addressed Adrian's strength, not some fault. A young man about to be expelled from school found a way to offer his gift. My friend, who shared the same interest, joined Adrian in realizing his dream of a bike shop. And, even better, the young man invited someone else he knew to share his gift.

Adrian had a talent and wanted—really wanted—to offer it. He loved working with his hands; he loved working on bicycles. He enjoyed collaborative efforts, like playing football. His problems with school went away as he focused more and more of his efforts on what he wanted to do, and he even found that people at school—students, teachers, and staff—were interested in who he was and what he was doing.

Everyone I meet has something that gives their life meaning, even if they don't think about it, or see it, in the moment. To find out what that something is doesn't take very long. It's as simple as changing the question, flipping the script, from asking "What's wrong with you?" to "How can I be a part of this thing that you love, and how can you share it with others?"

Shortly after the bicycle center got started, I received a call from someone at a development corporation on the opposite side of South Bend. They wanted to know if they could meet with the founders of the Major Taylor Bicycle Recycling Center and School. I drove the three of them over to the meeting. I was surprised when I heard what the development corporation wanted to talk about. The representatives pointed to the abandoned gas station across the street and asked if Adrian and his friends wanted to move the shop into it. They said the owner gave them the property, and they, having heard about the bicycle shop, thought the young people might be interested in the space.

In reply, Adrian and Co. said nothing. I asked a few questions. I tried to press the three to say something, but nothing came out of their mouths. I was embarrassed and a little angry with them.

On the drive back to their homes, I asked the guys what was wrong. One of them asked, "Who controls the money if we take their offer?"

I said, "Well, I suppose you do. But I don't know."

Then he asked about the development company's motivation. I told him what I thought to be the truth. I said, "I don't know. But all your life you're going to work with people whose motivations are unknown to you, and you'll have to figure out, whether you know the motivations or not, if you want to take them up on their offer."

One of the young men (who was fourteen years old at the time) piped up with the most practical question: How would they get over there in the winter? Winters are quite cold in South Bend, with a lot of snow. These guys rode their own bikes in warmer weather, but how would they get to the other side of town in winter? And then they said, "We want to stay in our own neighborhood." Now I understood their silence. On every level—practical, financial, and spiritual—it made more sense to stay where they were.

> Our neighborhoods are full of people, young and
> old, who are bakers and bicycle lovers and en-
> trepreneurs and artists and more. Our streets
> aren't dark and dangerous; they're bright and
> imaginative.

The next question held the biggest bombshell: "Don't they have any kids in their neighborhood?" This raised an issue that I wasn't thinking about at all. Of course, there were plenty of young people in that neighborhood. Why wasn't the development corporation listening to those kids and building on what they offered? Why, when looking for promising kids to invest in, did they go outside their own neighborhood?

Our neighborhoods are full of people, young and old, who are bakers and bicycle lovers and entrepreneurs and artists and more. If I could see my neighbors and their gifts, if I could shine a light on Adrian and his friends, others could see the same in their neighbors. Our streets aren't dark and dangerous; they're bright and imaginative.

Adrian and Co. continued to run the Major Taylor Center for years, until they were adults. It served them well. Years later, a group of young people in Ghana read their story and were inspired to start their own bicycle shop.

As I moved away from my fix-it mentality, I noticed that, more and more, I was walking and leaping and praising God. Peter and John—and Adrian, Fat Mike, Seana, and Aaron—were teaching me to trust the miracle waiting to leap out of the people I had thought needed help.

4

Getting Out of the Way

Never do something for someone that they can do for themselves. This was the "iron rule" our church heard from community organizers. I've heard this over and over, but it was in a hotel banquet room in Albany, New York, where I learned the rule's power. I was speaking to a group called the Mental Health Empowerment Project (MHEP) of the State of New York; in attendance were people who had been labeled mentally ill and their friends and families. When I gave my speech, I recited the rule. When the audience heard it, they stomped, cheered, and went wild. After the speech was over, I asked some of the attendees why they cheered so much for the rule. One answered, "Because no one ever lets us do anything."

The words hung in the air—and I think of them still, whenever I find myself lapsing into a mode of "helping" that doesn't make room for my neighbor's gifts.

Lucy's Flowers

One weekday morning a visitor stopped by the church. Her name was Lucy, and she wanted to know if she could do community service for us—she needed to complete forty hours as a condition of her parole. Short and black with a great smile, she was the soul of graciousness. When I asked Lucy what her crime was, it took her half an hour to tell me it was prostitution. She didn't want to tell me because she didn't think it was proper to talk about things like prostitution in the church building with the pastor. As I was thinking about what community service she might enjoy, I asked, "So, what are you good at?"

"I'm really good with people," Lucy said. (*Indeed*, I thought to myself.) We put her to work providing hospitality for all the people entering our church. Our building was very confusing: when someone came in the door, they would immediately encounter steps going up and down. And there were multiple places to go: the Head Start classrooms, the kitchen offering a daily senior citizens lunch, a thrift shop, an artists' studio, a food pantry, and a library. Lucy met people at the door, directed them to the right place, and got them a cup of coffee if they wished. But Lucy was still Lucy. After she finished her community service hours for the day, she spent the evening turning tricks.

Still, even after she completed her community service hours, Lucy stopped by the church office every couple of months for a cup of coffee and a visit. One time I asked her, "Lucy, if there was one thing you could do in the whole world, and money was no object, what would it be?" She said, "I'd really like to have a flower shop." I was surprised by her answer and responded, "Well, that's pretty unrealistic." But then I thought about it for a minute and told her, "Let's see what we can do."

It was a week before Valentine's Day, and Lucy and I went to a wholesale florist in the neighborhood and asked if we could buy $100 worth of flowers. The florist said, "Well, it's not really legal, but since you're the pastor. . . ." (I knew my seminary degree would come in handy at some point.) Then we went to the bank. I co-signed on the $100 loan—not because Lucy had bad credit, but because she had no credit. She'd never received a bill in her name in her life.

We borrowed the money and bought the flowers, and then Lucy and I went door-to-door in the neighborhood selling them just before Valentine's Day. We handed out cards that said "Lucy and the Rev's Flowers." We made $500, and she gave $50 to a day care center in the neighborhood. When I asked her why, she explained they were the caregivers for her daughter, who had been taken away from her by the state.

A week later, we went to repay the loan; for our week-long use of the bank's $100, we paid $117. The high payment was related to bank fees more than interest rate, but Lucy now had credit. I told her, "Okay! Now, for Mother's Day, we can borrow $500." But we didn't make it to Mother's Day that year. Lucy was arrested again as a habitual criminal and given a six-year sentence.

Three years later Lucy got out of prison early on "good time," and she headed back to the church. By now, we had created our own micro-lending fund called Lucy's Fund. Lucy borrowed $100 to order Easter lilies for the church. When she paid back the fund a few weeks later, she only had to pay back $101—as our fees were much lower than the bank's.

Lucy never got her own flower shop, but she did end up selling flowers out of her home to area churches. And she became a congregant—a helpful and delightful one—of our church.

What Do We Celebrate?

In 2007, when my family and I traveled to South Africa, I visited with the Rev. Welile Sigabi, the former minister of agriculture for the post-apartheid South African government. He was now a rural Methodist pastor. When he and I were standing in a parishioner's field, his anger flashed. "Here in South Africa, all liturgy is written by city people." I asked what he meant, and he replied, "In rural areas a man is not a man unless he has a cow. A woman is not a woman unless she has a chicken. Yet we have no liturgies to cel-

ebrate the births of cows and chickens." I saw that he was right;
the liturgies we write display our prejudices. They keep us blind
to what other people do and have.

Liturgies, whether religious ones written for holy worship or
secular ones written for daily life, most often strengthen our native
preferences (and prejudices). The songs and hymns we sing, the
Bible texts we read, and the prayers we offer encourage us to see
a world we already know. In the churches I led, we used liturgies
calling attention to the need and emptiness of people's lives, urg-
ing us to see the people around us as needy, broken, and "at-risk."
I didn't write or use liturgies gathering us together to celebrate
the remarkable wonder of God's glory shining on our inner-city,
low-income neighborhood.

Every grant application I filled out asked about the needs of
the neighborhood. In response, I would provide a litany of problems and needs: homelessness, juvenile delinquency, high rate of
teen pregnancy. One mentor told me that every grant application
after the first one had to argue, "Things got worse, but if you don't
give us this grant, things will be even more dire. So please give us
more money." Just another liturgy of need.

When I finally realized that abundance was all around us, I
began filling out grant applications differently. When a foundation
asked for the needs of our neighborhood, I wrote that our biggest
need was to be needed. If space was available, I provided a litany of the gifts of our neighbors and pointed out that our biggest
challenge was finding a way to keep up with all these gifts in our
neighbors' lives. So the grant application became a liturgy celebrating our neighbors.

We weren't saying that there weren't any needs. Those were
very clear and present, and we didn't have to turn over a rock to
find them. We were simply calling attention to a different problem—a better problem to have: How do we nurture the gifts
around us?

> When I finally realized that abundance was all
> around us, I began filling out grant applications
> differently. When a foundation asked for the
> needs of our neighborhood, I wrote that our big-
> gest need was to be needed. If space was available,
> I provided a litany of the gifts of our neighbors and
> pointed out that our biggest challenge was finding
> a way to keep up with all these gifts in our neigh-
> bors' lives.

When Charity Went Institutional

Several years ago, community organizer and professor John Mc-
Knight gave a speech relating a remarkable history. Talking with
his friend Ivan Illich, the sociologist, writer, and theologian, Mc-
Knight asked, "Ivan, when did everything start to go bad?"

"In a little Italian village in the eighth century," Ivan answered, and explained:

> In the little village, whenever a stranger knocked on a
> door, the stranger would be welcomed and given a place
> to stay and food to eat. In the eighth century, a monastery
> was built on the hill overlooking the village. And since
> it was a cloistered community, and they did not allow
> guests to stay with them, they built a little building on the
> back of the monastery, for the stranger. One of the peo-
> ple from the village learned about it and spread the word
> throughout the village. Afterwards, when the stranger
> would stop at someone's door, the citizens of the village
> would send the stranger to the monastery, to stay in the
> room behind the monastery. That was the first hostel.

And it was when the community gave away its power to care for one another.*

When charity becomes institutionalized, we forget that we can respond charitably to our neighbor. It's easy for the pastor of a church or a citizen walking down the street to refer a problem to an organization, but that's not always the best solution. When we take this route, we often give away our power to listen to and care for one another.

People who don't have much can do a lot. They have power and agency to act. That's why we don't use the term "empowered" around our church. Empowering people means to give people power. But people already have power—no one has to give it to them. By "empowering" people, we convince them by our actions and by our witness that they are in fact powerless.

When people believe they're powerless, efforts to help them often make matters worse. There's a medical term for it: *iatrogenesis,* meaning "help that hurts." Many social-service agencies and organizations and congregations make two significant mistakes. The first is not identifying the actual problem. The second is providing answers or remedies without talking with or involving those we intend to help. I know this from experience.

Broadway Church was one of the founders of the Mapleton—Fall Creek Housing Corporation, started in the mid-eighties. The organization's board was made up of representatives from the Protestant and Catholic churches in our neighborhood. One of their first projects, called "The Energy Forum," was to winterize some neighborhood homes. This grew out of the fact that many of the neighborhood congregations got daily requests from neighbors to help pay utility bills that were especially high in the wintertime. The housing corporation board thought that if we could

---

* From the John McKnight Speech, "My Friendship with Ivan Illich," at Broadway United Methodist Church, Indianapolis, Indiana, on April 6, 2009.

> When charity becomes institutionalized, we forget that we can respond charitably to our neighbor.

winterize homes, utility bills would be smaller, and there would be fewer urgent requests for help to pay them.

The board asked me to identify twenty-five homes for the project. I started by identifying the families who asked the church for utility assistance. Next, the board assigned a work team of volunteers from the neighborhood churches to winterize their homes. (In some cases, the residents of the homes in question were renters, not homeowners. Often, their landlords didn't raise a finger to fix the things that caused high utility bills.)

From one perspective, the project was a success: lots of volunteers gave time to help winterize homes, and donations of plastic sheeting, tape, caulk, and weather-stripping poured in. But from where I sit now, the project looks like a failure—it failed because it didn't ask the people who owned the homes or the people who lived in them to be part of solving the problem. We didn't ask landlords or the people living in the homes if they'd like to serve on the board of the housing corporation. We hired building contractors from across town to do some of the work, even though there were many people in our neighborhood who could have caulked around windows and taped plastic sheeting over unused doors. In my walks around the neighborhood, I had met many people with experience in construction, but it hadn't even occurred to me to invite them to join this project. One practical benefit of enlisting neighbors as partners would have been proximity: if something needed repair, a nearby neighbor could come by and take a look. Instead, we had work done by cross-town people whom the residents didn't know how to contact.

In short, a group of well-meaning do-gooders, myself included, winterized some homes—but in doing so, we stole a sense of agency from our neighbors. And many of the "helpers" came to resent the neighbors, whom they saw as absent and unwilling to help.

Like an Invading Army

I left the Energy Forum in Indianapolis, but soon after my move to South Bend I came face-to-face with something similar—the "Christmas in April" home repair program, a national program focused on inner-city neighborhoods. It gave Notre Dame students the chance to volunteer in the low-income communities around the city, helping fix up dilapidated houses. Our neighborhood was chosen as the next recipient of their service. Once we had been selected, city officials held a meeting of the congregations and social-service groups in our neighborhood to help identify homes where work was needed.

The city officials asked us to tell people in the neighborhood that the volunteers' appearance there was all right. "What do you mean?" I asked.

The city official replied, "People often view us as an invading army, and this perception has led to some tension in other neighborhoods where we've implemented this program. Could you just get the word out in the neighborhood that what we're doing is a good thing?"

I'd only been in the neighborhood a short time, but I already knew some neighbors were good at home repair. When I offered to connect these neighbors with the Christmas in April program, I was thanked but told that the program didn't need any more volunteers. They didn't want anyone from the neighborhood to help, not even to provide breakfast goodies and coffee to the workers on the service day. They already had everything covered.

So Christmas in April went on as planned in our neighborhood. It was easy to foresee the problems: young people with no skills in home repair, thirty assigned to each home, climbing all over the relatively small houses in the neighborhood. No wonder other neighborhoods felt the helpers were an invading army.

You Can't Build Anything with What You Don't Have

In the thirty years I've spent serving congregations in the city, I've been asked to fill out more than fifty needs surveys. Government agencies, private businesses, and non-profits have all wanted to know what needs existed in the neighborhood surrounding the church. The obvious problem was that they were asking me about needs rather than asking the people they were committed to serve. But a more basic problem emerged with these surveys: You can't build anything with what you don't have.

What you can do is build things with what is already in your hands. The citizens who live in low-income neighborhoods have many resources, gifts, and skills. If you want to lay good and strong foundations, build with what is present rather than what is not.

5

Making Sense of Money

In Indianapolis one of our interns went out into our neighborhood to record interviews with residents. He found himself talking to a woman in a car at the Double 8 grocery. He asked her what churches in the neighborhood should be doing.

"I don't have any idea," she said. "But I think they should give some of that money back!"

"What money?" he asked.

"All that money they got from runnin' those programs and not havin' to pay taxes, either. Things around here are all the same. And the preachers keep gettin' paid."

That isn't how I thought of my work. I thought I was living in response to Jesus's call. I thought I and my programs were the good news. When I looked around, though, I found it hard to disagree with the woman. In the previous twenty years in this Indianapolis neighborhood, things had not gotten better for most of the neighbors even as churches and a multitude of social service agencies had been very busy serving that community, providing services, training, and goods.

What to do? People from our parish began visiting with economists, physicians, and community developers around the country (and beyond), people who were thinking about how communities become healthier and economically stable and stronger. When we looked at efforts in Newark, New Jersey, and Malawi and in Brazil, we were inspired and challenged. What seemed to work best in these places were efforts that focused on building the gifts and the local wisdom and insight already there. The conversations we had encouraged us to take a bold step. We weren't going to talk about serving the poor anymore; we were going to talk about ending poverty.

For three months we put a banner in front of our church building that read "Ending Poverty" and then listed our worship times. We got a call from a city leader saying, "It's great that you're ending poverty at 8:30 and 10:45. What about the rest of the time?"

What were we doing about ending poverty? For decades, I'd been active helping out people who were poor (or as least I thought was helping). I'd fed the hungry. The churches I'd worked in had created after-school programs, summer programs, and tutoring programs. I'd helped set up computer labs and food pantries. I'd offered Thanksgiving baskets, Christmas gifts, and clothing.

I'd also participated in marches and protests to raise the minimum wage and to roll back laws that seemed to penalize the poor. My wife and I had sent our sons to public schools in the cities and neighborhoods in which we lived, and I'd been active in the schools, trying to make things better for my children's classmates.

I was a Matthew 25 Christian: feeding the hungry, clothing the naked, visiting the sick and those in prison. All of which I did. A lot.

While these things made me feel good, the train kept on rolling over the people I was serving. It even seemed to pick up steam as it moved down the tracks. And the tracks ran in one direction.

So, what was getting in the way of my making a real difference, really serving the poor? The problem was I saw the hungry as . . . well . . . only hungry. I saw those who needed clothing as

> For three months we put a banner in front of our
> church building that read "Ending Poverty" and
> then listed our worship times. We got a call from
> a city leader saying, "It's great that you're ending
> poverty at 8:30 and 10:45. What about the rest of
> the time?"

only naked. I paid more attention to the part of the text that said "feed and clothe" than to the part that called those I was serving sisters and brothers.

Today I'm still a Matthew 25 Christian. I just understand it differently.

Shoes and Silver Dollars

When I thought back on my own experience, I realized I had known something about financial hardship and how it affects people. When I was five years old, I walked into my parents' bedroom and found my mother, alone, with tears running down her face. "Mom? Why are you crying?"

"I don't have enough money to buy you and your brothers shoes."

I was confused. I had shoes. My brothers had shoes. I didn't know what Mom knew—that we were outgrowing them faster than her budget was keeping up. Her father had died when she was just five years old. So she knew what it was to live without having enough, and it frightened her.

My fierce, powerful, often angry mother was reduced to a quivering, quaking mess by this. Money is powerful. And the lack of it is even more powerful.

I think of the silver dollars pressed into my hand by people at the church when, at seven years old, I moved with my family from rural French Lick, Indiana, to a suburb of Indianapolis called Whiteland. I think of my early years in the pew when the offering was taken. I think of Mom giving me a dollar to put into the plate. It felt good to give.

One afternoon when I was ten, my parents handed me a few dollars, precious even in their small amount. For the very first time I was going to ride my bike to the school a quarter of a mile down the road and pay for my schoolbooks myself. I was proud and happy as I cycled that short distance away. But my happiness was short-lived. As I rode off the road and onto the great green of the school's lawn, I was pushed off my bike by an older boy. There was no one else around in the brightness of that ugly moment. He snatched the money out of my hand and rode off on his bicycle with the banana seat and the high handle bars. I was humiliated, bruised, and ashamed.

All of these experiences had taught me about the power of money. And yet, as I grew older, I divorced this life knowledge from my intereactions with the people I was living and working with who were poor. Now I saw that as a mistake. The truth is that money (and the lack thereof) is centrally connected to the every-day lives of people who are poor. They understand money's power, and they do talk about it.

Several years ago, I received an invitation from an Episcopal diocese in New England to speak to the members of what they call "outdoor congregations." These outdoor congregations were very different from the congregations who usually invited me to speak. Members of these congregations were people customarily referred to as homeless. I had been asked to talk with them about ending poverty. A young couple who had met on the street and married wanted to earn enough money to move into an apartment and begin building the life and family they dreamed about on summer nights on their backs in Boston Common. The husband already had an entrepreneurial gift: he could recycle almost anything into something that someone else would want to buy. A middle-aged Latin American immigrant talked quietly and expertly about the craft of making furniture. Who would hire him without legal papers? An older African-American woman sat softly humming through the first part of the conversation. At worship that afternoon, she led our gathered community in song, her voice rising. She knew how to lead, she knew how to inspire. Where could such gifts be rewarded?

What I saw was a great deal of innovation and wisdom for surviving in a way that would have made my own ineptitude shine through. These people didn't need training. They needed others to recognize their gifts and find places where they were valued.

We didn't solve the problem of poverty. We worshiped and ate together; we even spent the night on the floor of the cathedral together. The participants left remembering the good work they were capable of doing. If institutions, including the church, can see those gifts in the lives of those who are poor, the road out of poverty is built.

In faith communities, we're often more interested in helping people than in seeing equality achieved. We're more interested in seeing ourselves as the helping ones than in re-ordering the social order so that there are fewer people desperate for help.

And this isn't limited to the faith communities. In newspapers and on television and on Twitter, people talk about poverty. They talk about responding to people who live in poverty—providing educational services, allocating resources (i.e., food and clothing), delivering emergency bill assistance. National and international columnists recommend ways we can serve the poor. But rarely does anyone write about what can be done to end poverty.

For me, this has been, and is, one of the the most important thought shifts to make: to stop thinking about ameliorating the ravages of poverty and to think instead about ending poverty.

> In faith communities, we're often more interested
> in helping people than in seeing equality achieved.
> We're more interested in seeing ourselves as the
> helping ones than in re-ordering the social order
> so that there are fewer people desperate for help.

Money, Money, Money

I had learned my lessons well. Poverty was about making bad decisions and having a lousy education; it was about early pregnancy and drug addiction; it was about mental health and family structure. Sure, injustice was a part of it. I just wasn't sure how. But if I ran programs that made the givers feel good and that the poor showed up for, I must be on the right track.

I'd missed the simple point that being poor means you don't have money.

I've worked in low-income communities in New Jersey and Indiana. In each place, we established a wide range of programs and services. In each we provided summer programs for young people that included art, history, music, Bible study, poetry, math, and more. We provided a wealth of services and opportunities, but not money. *Because,* I thought to myself, *It isn't about money.* I thought it was about all the other things missing in the lives of the poor.

While in South Bend, I got invited to a press conference at the St. Joseph County Health Department, which was releasing the results of a five-year study. It reported that people who don't have money are less healthy than people who have money. All but two of the people in the room were health-care professionals. They offered different ideas about programs their institutions could provide to improve the health of people who don't have much money—even though that wasn't the point of the study. And then they proposed programs through which they paid themselves to deliver services to poor people.

At least one of the proposals should have focused on finding a way for poor people to get more money. The issues raised by this study and the attendees' tone-deaf response to it challenged me more than any situation I had struggled with before. I could hear my mother say to me (as she did so often), "Just use a little common sense, Mike." Common sense would say: Find ways to get money into the hands of those who don't have much of it.

The lack of money was the biggest challenge I dealt with daily as people stopped by to request help from me in the church office. They didn't have enough money to prevent themselves from being evicted from a home, having their gas or lights turned off, or having no affordable transportation.

The lack of money isn't determinative, but it's very powerful. People in the charter school movement often say, "Poverty isn't destiny." They're right. But back in the 1930s, '40s, and '50s, people would say, "Segregation isn't destiny." They were right, too. You could point to Mary McLeod Bethune, Martin Luther King Jr., and Paul Robeson—a few among many others who rose from the prison of segregation. But most who lived under segregation were held in check by it.

Segregation legally locked out black and brown people from access to jobs, services, citizenship, and equal education. Poverty locks people out of opportunity. Studies show that as a group, people with less money find *in every way* that their futures are more limited than those of people with more money. The single most determinative factor affecting high school graduation rates, health, and employment is economic status (income and net worth). And most efforts to "help" those in poverty have very little impact on this most powerful of factors.

When I helped someone with their rent or utility bills, I staved off for a month or two the eviction or the loss of access to the service. That's not nothing—but it's palliative rather than healing.

And those who consider themselves "helpers" often become resentful that people aren't changing and "getting better." For decades I sat in meetings where people running food pantries talked non-stop about those receiving food as untrustworthy or worse. Those discussions both reflect and shape the perspective of the "helpers," making it nearly impossible for them to see the gifts of the people they're trying to help.

Some clergy and laity from an inner-city church in the Midwest visited us recently. These leaders explained how their congregation offered "giveaways"—but then complained that many of the people who came to them "took too much." I asked how that could be, since I was pretty sure that people weren't taking more than they were being given. They weren't. But the volunteers and the staff at the church still felt like people were taking more than they needed. And they resented those who received their charity.

Our church and community began asking ourselves a set of new questions. For instance, we asked how we could use money to reveal the power and abundance we witnessed in others. We began to notice a subtle shift that moved us from asking how we could help to how we could become venture capitalists. Where could we invest our money in this neighbor? What services or products that these gifted entrepreneurs offered could we multiply by helping them share their paintings, poetry, fishing talent, jewelry, carpentry, and more?

We knew our neighbors still needed money to pay their bills, but we would now focus on the talents and gifts each person had to offer, and how those gifts could help them get more money. When a neighbor stopped by to ask for assistance in paying for school expenses for the grandsons she was raising, she was carrying a beautifully handcrafted purse. A church member noticed and asked where she got it. She said that she had made it, and went on to describe in intricate detail the craft of purse-making. When we asked if she had any more, she brought us three she had made; we paid her for them and used them as gifts for a church fundraiser.

What she had to offer made other people happy, and it made her happy. And it made her money.

As we focused more and more on the gifts of people around us, we stopped collecting money for emergency assistance. We created a new account and called it "The Abundance Fund." We don't use money from this fund to pay utility or rent bills. We use The Abundance Fund to pay people to share their gifts with others.

When people request emergency assistance, they're taken aback when we tell them we can't pay their bill. But when we ask if they're willing to have a conversation, no one ever says "No." We ask what they care about. We ask what they do when no one else is watching, when they're doing something they don't have to do. We ask what others say about them. What do the people who love them say they're best at? If it's something practical—if they make a product or provide a service—we offer to try it and pay them for it.

We use this as an opportunity to build community and to reveal the abundance of community through the investment of our money. When we give money to people who have shared this gift with us, we encourage their sharing that gift with others. Because we invest in them, we both see and remember what they have to offer.

As we changed our response to people's requests for help, we began to notice other changes. We noticed a shift in how people felt as they left the church offices. When we were paying people's bills, they often left with the same posture with which they arrived. Head down. Spirits down. Now people often leave smiling, even though they still have no money in their pockets. The change has been astonishing.

One of the first people who came to us as we were changing our questions told us she was a good baker and that she made great cookies. So we bought some from her, and they were delicious. Based on our tasting experience, we asked her to make some for a neighbor who was ill and who loved cookies. We offered to pay her to make the cookies, take the cookies to her neighbor, and

> As we focused more and more on the gifts of people around us, we stopped collecting money for emergency assistance. We created a new account and called it "The Abundance Fund." We don't use money from this fund to pay utility or rent bills. We use The Abundance Fund to pay people to share their gifts with others.

visit with her. Paying the baker for her work was the point, *and* getting two neighbors to meet and share together was the point. The "helpers" of the church didn't have to put themselves in the center of this "assistance." The baker never mentioned our encouragement of her, or our paying her, and that was perfect.

Next a singer came into the church's office. She loved an audience. Where could she find one? Every afternoon when the bus dropped students off at a corner near her home, the bus stop was packed. So she stood in an empty lot near the stop and began to sing, and we paid her for it. The young women and men, who included her sons, turned and stared. But soon they were clapping, and some joined her in song. When she told us the story, she leaned back and laughed. A couple of years later, she sang "His Eye Is on the Sparrow" at the funeral of a family member of one of those young people who met her at the bus stop. Since then, the funeral home has hired her to sing for more funerals.

Another woman made clothes for children. By showing other church members and neighbors some examples of her work, we expanded her customer base. We also met a man who was a good auto mechanic, and we directed church members and neighbors who needed car repair to him.

It often takes a while to really discover people's gifts. That was true for us, because when we first started asking people what they were good at, they didn't believe we really wanted to know. Some believed they still needed to tell us the best story about how bad things were—the worse, the better. Now the script was flipped; we were asking for a different story. And different stories emerged. Slowly at first, but then they began pouring out.

And the gifts that we discovered multiplied. We were pleased to see that neighbors reached out to each other more often. And neighbors who used the gifts of other neighbors began to see the abundance that was both around them and within themselves. Also, when people from outside the neighborhood went "inside" and hired someone to cook a meal, or bought a piece of art, or got their nails done, they began to see ostensibly needy people as artists, economists, musicians, chefs, and entrepreneurs.

Cultivating Joy

I was still struggling to see how to grow this giftedness in ways that put more money into the hands of my neighbors. Right around that time my colleagues and I noticed that there were a number of empty lots around the neighborhood; the obvious question was, Why not create a community garden? People around here needed to eat healthier food, so a garden would help, right? (The people of Broadway have always been ahead of the trends, creating the first community garden back in the late eighties.)

I thought people didn't know how to garden because they were poor, so I recruited people from the School of Agriculture at Purdue University to teach gardening. When I came back to Indianapolis in 2003, the community garden still limped along, and a smaller one had been added a block away. Both were maintained by church employees.

In his work as a roving listener for the church, De'Amon was getting neighborhood reports of people who loved gardening. In fact, within a five-block area around Broadway, he discovered forty

70

gardeners. People had gardens in their front yards, back yards, and side yards, on their front porches and inside their houses. When I began the community garden effort earlier, I hadn't even noticed the gardens or the gardeners. Now De'Amon pointed them out, and suggested a way to begin acting on what we were seeing: hire two neighborhood young people to go talk with all the gardeners, the ones already identified and others they discovered along the way. It was an excellent idea. The young people asked the gardeners what they grew, what they did with it, if they were interested in selling any of it, and, if so, how would they like to distribute their produce (through a central drop-off location, a delivery to the consumer, or a pick up at their home and garden)?

Then the young people went to the institutions, businesses, and associations in our neighborhood to see who was interested in purchasing food from neighborhood gardeners. The youth also asked potential customers how they would like to get the food: delivered to a central location, dropped off at their home or work, or picked up at the gardener's home?

We expected this garden project to be a several-year process. We thought the young people could build connections between those who were growing and those who were interested in buying. If it meant creating a farmers' market, that would be fine. If it meant that gardeners would deliver produce to people's homes, that would be fine. If it meant that buyers would go to a gardener's home and pick up their order, that would be fine, too.

Around the time the young people started surveying the gardeners, my oldest son, Conor, returned home from his first year of college—it was early summer in 2008. The first evening he was home, he sat with his mother and me and told us he had been getting confused lately. He had gone to dinner with his friends the night before, and when the waitress came and asked what he wanted to drink, he couldn't even think of the word "water," and when she asked what he wanted to eat, he realized he wasn't able to read the menu. He asked for the chicken, but she didn't seem to understand, so he pointed at the picture of the chicken in the menu. She brought his food and he ate, quietly. When he looked around at the friends he was sitting with, he realized he couldn't recall any of their names. After dinner he paid his bill and left and went to bed. But when he got up the next morning, everything was fine. He told us he just thought he should mention what had happened.

Kathy and I were scared, but we tried to be as calm as he was. The next morning we took him to our family physician. She scheduled him for an MRI that afternoon, and by the end of the day we knew he had a brain tumor in the language and thought part of his brain. Our lives were turned upside down. What was going to happen? What would his future be?

The surgery was scheduled for June 27. Two weeks before, the neurosurgeon called Conor and told him CNN wanted to do a story about his brain surgery. (Ted Kennedy had recently been diagnosed with a brain tumor, and the hospital saw Kennedy's diagnosis as an opportunity to publicize its work in brain surgery.) Conor, a shy young man, said no. A couple of days later, we went to see the neurosurgeon in preparation for the surgery, and he encouraged Conor to revisit the possibility of sharing his story. The surgeon said he thought it would be helpful for audiences to hear from a "normal nineteen-year-old college kid from the Midwest" who was having this procedure done. He said people were afraid to have it, but it was dangerous not to have it, and Conor might be able to help. Conor said, "But *I* am afraid to have the surgery!"

A few days later Conor decided he was willing to talk with CNN, but he wanted me to talk with some people at the hospital first and make a request. So I met with the vice president, telling him that Conor would share his story but only if the hospital promised to do some of these surgeries for free for people who couldn't afford them otherwise.

The vice president agreed to Conor's request, and as we continued talking, he said to me, "I hear good things about your church. What's going on over there?" Even though my mind was filled with thoughts about Conor, I had met earlier that day with the young people who were talking with the gardeners, so I told the vice president about their work. He got very excited and said, "Wow! Could they do a farmers' market here at the hospital?"

"No," I replied.

"No?"

"No. The young people are just getting started. This will take several years and will require laying a foundation and doing organizing work."

He said, "We'd have seed money for that." I thought, *Great. Fifty bucks for seeds.* Then he said, "$40,000."

Conor spoke to CNN, had the surgery, and came through it well. He returned to those friends he could name and finished college, graduating three years later. Meanwhile, the hospital came through with their promise to provide a number of brain surgeries at no cost. And the hospital invested $40,000 in the gardeners of our "poor" neighborhood, and every penny went to the neighborhood organizers for gathering and working with their gardener neighbors. As I type this, the gardeners from our neighborhood are working with the hospital to ensure that they're meeting the various health codes and providing the business licenses required to sell food on hospital property.

If the church had continued to run the community gardens program the way we'd done for twenty years, the opportunity for the hospital to invest in our neighbors never would have materialized. And the church would still be maintaining and caring for the community gardens that no one really wanted.

De'Amon's work opened my eyes to the return on investment (De'Amon calls it "return on community") that is always present. Our neighbors' green beans and tomatoes and zucchini were growing right in front of us—we just needed the eyes to see them. Conor's brain tumor was nobody's opportunity, but

> If the church had continued to run the community
> gardens program the way we'd done for twenty
> years, the opportunity for the hospital to invest in
> our neighbors never would have materialized. And
> the church would still be maintaining and car-
> ing for the community gardens that no one really
> wanted.

others ended up seeing the growing abundance in our neighborhood. When I look back, the way everything came together
makes sense to me.

Cultivating Imagination

I had been trained to offer programs providing services to the poor
and needy—but what if the people who the programs "served"
could be hired to run them? In 2003, Seana Murphy, the young
woman who told me in 1986 that she was going to be the next
Martin Luther King Jr., was leading the 21st Century Scholars Program for the state of Indiana, which gave college tuition support
to high-achieving, low-income students.

When Seana took over the program, it employed people in
almost every county in the state. She told her staff that whenever
a job came open, she wanted them to hire the parent of a child in
her program. This was brilliant on two counts: (1) Everyone in the
program was low-income, and those jobs could be life-changing;
and (2) no one cared more about the young people in the program
than their parents.

What if all programs were managed with this kind of imagination? Seana looked at the parents and saw people who had some-

thing to contribute to make the program successful. Seana saw the gifts of those who others saw as under-resourced or needy because she knew that her mother, though poor, was a remarkable woman who knew how to do exactly what she wanted those running her program to do.

Seana revealed not only that paying attention changes everything you do and how you do it—but that *how you do things carries more weight than what you think*. The AA recovery mantra is right: "We don't think our way into new ways of acting; we act our way into new ways of thinking." Unfortunately, we often act in ways that reinforce our old understandings. Seana's staff, all good public servants, had a hard time wrapping their minds around hiring the people they were committed to serve. "Is this really the right thing to do?" they asked. "Why are parents important?" (Seana assured them that yes, it was the right thing, and that parents, though often disregarded or disrespected by our social service network, know more about their children and care more about them than an army of degreed professionals.)

Seana continued her good work for ten years. During those years she put the leadership of this state agency into the hands of the families of those they were serving. When she first arrived, the staff ran workshops twice a year. By the time she left, those workshops were run and staffed by the parents of young people in the program. When the "experts" and "professionals" ran the workshops, they were very poorly attended. When parents ran them, they filled the hotels where meetings were held. Those parents now speak all over the country, telling the story of what they're doing for their own families and the other families in our state.

The Incarnation and Money

Over the years, I have become more convinced of the central role that money plays in almost every aspect of our lives: in our rela-

> Seana revealed not only that paying attention
> changes everything you do and how you do it—but
> that *how you do things carries more weight than what
> you think.* The AA recovery mantra is right: "We
> don't think our way into new ways of acting; we
> act our way into new ways of thinking."

tionships, in our life in our neighborhoods, in our churches, and in our workplaces.

Jesus came to the world in an embodied presence. He talked about concrete things, like money, a lot. Money is something that shows people what we value in our society. Money is a tool—a powerful tool.

My professors in seminary didn't spend much time talking about the economic difficulties that people faced, except to encourage us to pray for people and to counsel them through financial difficulties. What caused my whole world to change—what caused all the unlearning and then the relearning—was realizing that I could use money to support the gifts, talents, and dreams of people whom I had thought of as needy.

Most of us remember Jesus's instruction to the rich young ruler in Matthew 19:21: "If you would be perfect, go, sell your possessions, and give the money to the poor, and you will have treasure in heaven." This familiar line looks new to me through my more recent experiences. Maybe the best way to give to the poor is by using the resources in our own hands and endowing them in the lives of the very people they're intended to help.

6

Practicing Hospitality

It was beautiful and sunny, a late summer afternoon in 1970. My youngest brother, Alan, was riding his bicycle in front of our house. He was six.

I don't know if I heard the crash. But I know everything sped up. My mother ran out the front door, and I could hear her call out, "Someone get help!" I saw a car, my brother's bike lying in the street, and several people gathered around.

Not me. I stayed on the porch. I was scared to move. Scared to see what had happened. The panic and the late summer heat from the street rolled toward me. The next thing I knew, the babysitter came to stay with us while Mom and Dad went with Alan in the ambulance to the hospital.

The babysitter got a phone call from my parents. "I could hear Alan screaming in the background," she said, as the doctors put him in a salt bath to clean the skin scraped off one side of his body. I wasn't on the phone line, but even now, I hear his screams.

Two days later it was Alan's birthday. We were all at the kitchen table—Alan too. He was bandaged, but present. The meal was finished, and the cake was coming. The humidity of the Indiana summer made the air thick and our sweat plentiful.

Just before we started singing, there was a knock at the front door, and Dad excused himself to answer it. I heard muffled voices, but we kids weren't paying attention. This kind of thing happened often, because we lived in the parsonage next door to the church. We just waited for Dad to come back.

When he walked back toward the kitchen, a young man was beside him. Not yet twenty, he wore his gloom like a yoke. His head was bent. He carried a hat, like a fig leaf, in front of him. He was the driver of the car that hit Alan, he told us, and he wanted to apologize.

Alan accepted the apology quickly. What he wanted was some cake. And he wasn't mad anyway. The accident was two whole days ago! Mom said to the young man, "Please stay and have some cake with us. It's Alan's birthday."

He hung his head lower. He said he couldn't, but Mom and Dad insisted. Slowly he lowered himself into a chair. Then he joined in as we sang "Happy Birthday" to a boy we were all happy was alive. The first piece of cake went to Alan, the second piece to our guest. I don't remember any other cake from my childhood. But I remember that one.

One of the rules around Broadway is "Practice hospitality." It's more than handing out umbrellas to keep church members dry when they walk from the sanctuary to their cars in the rain. It's more than taking a gift to a newcomer or dropping in at the home of someone who has visited the church. Hospitality is creating a welcome place at the table. And it's recognizing that the other, the outsider, the visitor, is one's sister or brother, one of the family.

It took me a long time to remember my parents' welcome— but eventually it became my template for hospitality. I had begun asking myself, *What does it mean to truly welcome the people who come to see me with a request for help? What does it mean to truly welcome our neighbors who we're beginning to see as gifted people?*

I learned about hospitality from my parents, but I also learned about hospitality by hearing Sam, a former church intern, tell the

> Hospitality is creating a welcome place at the table. And it's recognizing that the other, the outsider, the visitor, is one's sister or brother, one of the family.

story of our church to his home church. After his internship ended, Sam began talking with folks at his home church about Broadway's work of paying attention to people's gifts. Someone asked him, "If I find out somebody loves to go fishing, what program do I connect them to?"

He responded, "If I told you I loved to go fishing, you wouldn't say, 'Boy, do I have a program for you!' You'd say, 'When are you going fishing again? Can I go along? What do you do with the fish you catch? Why haven't you invited me over to eat some of the ones you've caught?'"

Sam captured the true spirit of hospitality. True hospitality draws people together. It doesn't refer people to someone or somewhere else.

Going Beyond the Youth Group

Duane Carlisle, a long-time church member, joined our staff in 2007 as the Pastor for Children, Youth, and Families, and was another mentor to us in practicing hospitality.

When he first came on staff, we told Duane, "If you start a youth group, you're fired." We were serious. We didn't want a new youth group. We wanted to build on the gifts of the youth in our parish and were looking for fresh ways to discover those gifts and callings.

Duane began his work by setting up celebration meals for the individual youths in our parish. At each meal, the young person's family would be present as the most important and powerful teachers and presences in his or her life. Bringing them to the table acknowledged that relationship. The youth also invited his or her friends to the meal. These individuals, whether adults or other young people, often saw things in their friend that the family hadn't noticed. The affirmation of the youth by friends and family bound those two groups closer together in support of this person they knew and loved. And Duane also invited an individual or two who he thought would connect well with the young person—people who had the same interest or gift as the young person, people who he or she might or might not already know.

When the meal was over, Duane would invite everyone to tell the youth what giftedness or calling each saw in his or her life. As the affirmations poured out, you could see the young person's confidence blossoming.

Then the youth was asked to speak about his or her own sense of calling or giftedness. Sometimes he or she talked about a dream for his or her life. This was a powerful moment, because in many cases the youth had never mentioned this to a family member or a friend. Naming one's calling, one's dream, out loud brought clarity and direction to the comments already offered.

At this point, Duane would go around the room once more and ask if anyone present had something they were willing to contribute to support the gifts and dreams of the young person. At that moment, remarkable things happened. At one such meal, a young woman surprised everyone by talking about her love for opera. As it turned out, one of the other people in the room was a singer in the local opera company. He asked her if she would like a tour of the local opera house and suggested that the two of them could sing an operatic duet at worship later that year.

In the final action of the meal, everyone would gather around and lay hands on and bless the youth. This action, deeply rooted in Christian tradition, embodied what had just happened in words. It joined together young and old in the common work of supporting, appreciating, and blessing each other.

Montell, who lives in our neighborhood but doesn't attend our church, was one of several youth to talk with the church's governing board about his celebration meal. Montell's grandmother, mother, brother, and sister had attended, as well as a man who had been his tutor years before, and a teacher Montell was close to. Montell's grandmother spoke about his care for her. She uses a wheelchair, and Montell gets her out of bed every morning and prepares her to face the day ahead. She talked about his gentleness in caring for her. His mother and brother shared personal stories about his stubbornness and perseverance when he had been discounted at school and other places in the community. His tutor and his teacher talked about his inquisitiveness and interest in learning.

When it came time for Montell to share, he talked about his dream of one day having his own place where old people were cared for with dignity. The people around the room, including his family, were stunned. No one had known that this was his dream. Some offered to invest in him. His tutor said, "Montell, I'd like to take you to visit a few places that are known for treating people with dignity and gracious care." Others mentioned people they knew who were involved in this kind of work and said they could introduce him. Not surprisingly, all the people in the room were crying as they laid hands on Montell and blessed him.

After Montell and others shared stories of their celebration meals, the governing board of the church asked, "Why do we do this just for youth? Everyone should have this experience." Yes!

What's the Agenda?

Broadway Church is a teaching congregation—we mentor seminary students each year. One of the ways we try to help these students learn the power of hospitality is to include in their job description the responsibility to, once a month, organize and attend a meal with people who all care about the same thing.

When I first mentioned this, an intern interrupted me. "The dinner idea is great. But what's the agenda?"

"You're not going to have to worry about that," I answered. "They all care about the same thing. They're going to talk with each other."

Another seminarian responded to the assignment by saying, "I don't think of this as ministry." I had heard that before. Many seminarians feel that ministry is leading Bible study, visiting people in the hospital, and leading worship. It is those things, yes, but it's also gathering people together who otherwise would never meet but who all care about the same thing and share similar talents and interests. Every meal would be a time when like-minded people were attentive to one another and the gifts they brought to the table.

We asked the students to pay attention to where the energy in the room was going and then come back and tell us what they saw. One month they told us about the neighbor who gathered artists together around a meal. Mashed potatoes, green beans, and chicken became the fuel of the Spirit. Over apple crisp people discovered mutual delight and learned from one another.

One night this past summer, four meals were going on at once. In the upstairs apartment of a fairly new low-income highrise in our neighborhood, people who were raising children with autism gathered to share stories. One of the people at the table had started a school for autistic children after her two sons couldn't find a place in the public schools in their suburban school district. Mothers talked with each other about raising their children, shared resources they had discovered, and made plans to visit the school the one parent had started. They found comfort that evening in sharing their lives.

At another home, people got together to talk about the recent shooting by a white supremacist at an African-American church in Charleston, South Carolina. In this home, which doubles as a day care center, families and children came and went while the

> These individuals, who hadn't met before, then
> began to talk across the boundaries our society
> puts up between races, and decided to continue
> the conversation after the meal and the evening
> were over.

people who had gathered talked about the grief, anger, and hope they were feeling. They prayed together about their concerns for the people of Charleston and the people of this nation. These individuals, who hadn't met before, then began to talk across the boundaries our society puts up between races, and decided to continue the conversation after the meal and the evening were over.

Less than a block away, a group of musicians, painters, and fabric artists gathered to talk about their love of art. Most of them had never met before, though many lived within a few blocks of each other. One woman got up and sang for the group. Others shared pictures of art pieces they had made. Another artist had brought along one of his pieces, carried on the bicycle he rode everywhere. Several artists told the gathering about opportunities to submit art proposals around the city.

At another house pulsing with life, photographers from the neighborhood, from outside the neighborhood, and even from outside our city gathered to share photos with one another and compare equipment and techniques. One of the photographers shepherded the group out to the front sidewalk and pointed at an abandoned house across the street where life-size photographs had been put up that day, covering the doors and windows. As he was telling the story of these images to the other photographers, neighbors stopped by to talk. One of them asked, "Could someone come and take a picture of me at my job?" Others asked if their photographs could be taken and put up on other homes around the neighborhood.

Meals and meetings can become places where hospitality is practiced and people are brought more deeply into relationship with one another. One night around a dinner table at De'Amon's home, a group of artists had gathered to get to know one another. As they were talking, one of them pointed out the black band tattooed on the arm of the young man next to him. The band was visible even against the dark caramel of his skin. The young man paused, took a breath, and said, "I struggle with depression. Last year was the first year in a long time that I didn't try to commit suicide. I tattooed this band on my arm so that I would remember that I can go for a whole year without trying to kill myself." The room was quiet. Then the man who had noticed the tattoo said, "I get depressed too." At this point, others around the table joined in talking about the experience of depression in their own life or the life of someone they knew and loved. New friendships were born as people shared not only the suffering but the hope around the table.

Sometimes Hospitality Begins with Saying No

My parents had said yes to the young man who showed up at our door after my brother's accident. But sometimes hospitality begins with saying no.

A woman named Frances had come to the church seeking help. Her house had been in the line of fire in a drive-by shooting, and a bullet had burrowed into her house and into her leg. (She came to us after she had been treated for her gunshot wound.) She didn't want to stay at the house anymore, she told us, and she wondered if we could put her up in a hotel for a few nights. We said no, but we also asked if she could stay and talk, and she agreed. When we first asked Frances if she knew anyone who could take her in, she told us there was no one. But then, as we talked, she said, "You know, I have a cousin who lives nearby. I

haven't talked with her for a while. Maybe she would take me in."
She called her cousin from the church, and she said she would be
happy to have Frances stay with her. Hospitality is often available,
if only we ask for it.

We asked Frances to come back to see us once she got set-
tled, and she came by several days in a row for conversation.
When one of our custodians was talking with her, she mentioned
that none of her neighbors at the house that had been shot up
cared about her. A day later the custodian was walking by her
old house, and one of the neighbors called out to him and asked
if he knew where Frances was staying. When he asked why, she
told him that she and several other neighbors were concerned
about how Frances was doing. The woman mentioned that she
had been picking up Frances's mail and wondered if he knew
how to get it to her.

The custodian asked if she'd be willing to gather other neighbors to come down for lunch at the church on Friday, and she said
yes. He didn't tell Frances about this—he just invited her to meet
him at the church for lunch on Friday. When Frances walked into
the room and saw that it was full of her neighbors, she burst into
tears. Her friends surrounded her, laughing and talking, getting
caught up. She thought they didn't care for her. Now she knew
they did.

A month later, Frances was getting back on her feet and asked
a staff member at the church if she could volunteer by answering
phones in the office. As she worked, she had conversations with
church members who found out she was a good cook. They hired
her to make lunch for a few of them and loved it, so they hired
her to provide one of our monthly meals after worship on Sunday.
Now Frances cooks lunch every day in a commercial kitchen in a
church in our neighborhood. Neighbors, visitors to the neighborhood, church staff, and church members all take advantage of her
fine cooking—a gift that was discovered through the hospitality
that began with "No."

Birthday cakes and gunshots and life-size photographs—as far as I could tell, my colleagues in other congregations weren't thinking about hospitality and community life in the ways my neighborhood was pushing me to think. I needed to talk with other people about this. People who were thinking about community, economy, and mutual delight. People I could learn from, people we could learn with.

7

Taking Learning Journeys

Over Christmas break of my freshman year in college (1977) at the University of Evansville, a couple of my fellow music majors and I hit the road. In those days I wanted to be a professional jazz trumpet player, and we were driving to a jazz convention in Dallas. I especially wanted to meet Dizzy Gillespie, who I heard was accompanying a college jazz band there on its winter tour.

In Dallas I wandered the halls of the convention. In mid-afternoon I saw some old guys practicing in the empty hotel bar and stepped in to listen. (At eighteen, I was too young to be in a bar when it was open. I had to take my chances when I got them!) And then, amazingly enough, Dizzy Gillespie walked in. His trademark trumpet in his hand (bell lifting at an angle from the horizontal lines of the trumpet as if playing to the heavens), he took the bar stool next to me. The men in the band quickly recognized him and rushed over. Dizzy regaled us all with stories and one-liners. He said something that I didn't understand then, but it stayed with me: "It's taken me all my life to learn what not to play."

The line returned with greater clarity years later, at that Pentecost Community Dinner in South Bend: when I was challenged to consider why we didn't treat people like they had something to offer, I understood that I was being asked to learn what not to

play. When we stopped doing the summer program in Indianapolis and tried something different, I was learning what not to play.
So Dizzy's lesson at the bar not only changed my life; it began
changing the lives of women and men, young and old, coming
into contact with the congregations I served. Adele opened Adelita's Fajitas because I was learning what not to play. Men and
women in our neighborhood in Indianapolis have made more
money, taught classes, and gotten healthier because I've learned
what not to play.

After meeting Dizzy Gillespie, I began intentionally reaching
out to those doing important, interesting work that I could learn
from. If an author wrote a book that stimulated me, I would call
or write and ask for a conversation. When I was in the middle of a
conversation with someone who struck me as important, I asked
them if they knew of others whom I should try to engage on these
questions or ideas. And if they did, I asked if they would write me
"a Victorian letter of introduction."

The learning journeys I've taken are all like the one I made to
that 1977 jazz convention—efforts to seek out wisdom from and
with those more skilled and knowledgeable than I. And the learning journeys are, in their way, jazz compositions. I take a melody,
a tune, from someone whose notes sound similar to the notes I'm
inclined to play, and I jam with them. I don't know where our conversation is going to lead or what I'm going to learn, but I always
learn something.

Learning from a Tiny Town

In the late 1990s I met Maria Varela in Los Ojos, a small, low-
income village in northern New Mexico. Maria had come there
in the sixties as a worker for SNCC (the Student Non-Violent Co-
ordinating Committee). Her job was to organize a health clinic in
this poorest of counties in the United States. A few years later she

had a child, which enabled her to have more personal encounters with the other mothers in the village. These encounters gave her an intimate view of how her neighbors lived. Among other things, she saw the women make beautiful clothing, rugs, and tablecloths for their families and homes.

Those stunning objects gave Maria an idea, and she built on that like a musician would follow chord progressions on a jazz chart. Families raised sheep here, then sold the wool to be processed and made into yarn and re-sold by others. Once the wool left Los Ojos, it never returned. Maria knew that the shepherds could make more money if they processed the wool themselves and cut out the middle man. With her encouragement, the women began to do that, and Maria found herself wondering why they shouldn't move forward by making the yarn and selling it. The next progression was equally clear, and the women began to sell the products they were making with the yarn.

When I visited in the late 1990s, the little village—which had only one street—boasted an upscale store where the women sold the things they made. Behind the store stood the factory—owned by the women of the county—where the women processed their wool and then began turning it into beautiful products. Each item in the store had a tag attached that introduced the woman who had made it and told a little piece of her story.

For this work, Maria won the MacArthur Genius Grant, so it was on to her next progression. She took the money and used it to build a computer lab in Los Ojos, and she staffed it with middle-school-aged children. She had noticed that it was young people who knew how to use computers.

Maria's work inspired our congregation to think both about the economic possibilities in our low-income neighborhood and about the power of young people. We took a close look at the resources surrounding us, and we thought about how to invest in them. One such resource was the neighborhood library—it was a real jewel in the county library system. It sat on the farthest boundary of our neighborhood, and several of the librarians told us they rarely saw any of our neighbors there.

In December of 2000, a church member and I visited a family who had signed up for Christmas help. During our visit, the college-age daughter told us about her love of books. Shortly after that, while walking past the library on a snowy day, I had an idea: Maria had hired young people to lead in Los Ojos, and we could do the same in our neighborhood. So we hired the young woman to lead her neighbors in walking to the library at noon and in the evening. She was the Pied Piper, and the crowd behind her grew as she walked. As these neighbors walked, they talked. It turned out that one of them was a cheesemaker, and others started placing orders with him. One of them got a job delivering the cheese to distributors in Atlanta. Another neighbor with an in-home restaurant invited fellow walkers to her home to eat, and two more of these in-home restaurants opened that summer.

People often talk about how young people are the future. Maria gave me eyes to see that young people are ready to lead now.

Try the Realistic Solution

On another learning journey, this one in 2007, I visited Rev. Charles Villa-Vicencio, who had worked with the Truth and Reconciliation Commission in South Africa. Over tea, he said to me, "We had a joke in South Africa in the eighties. 'There are two possible solutions to our crises here. One is miraculous, and one is realistic. One solution is that God will send down angels and sort us all out. That's the realistic solution. The miraculous one is that we will sit down and talk with our enemies.'"

What does it look like to live as if I believe in the miraculous solution? What does it look like to live as if the gospel were true? These were questions I continued to ask when I was in South Africa. And I asked them when visiting with Father Peter-John

Pearson, who at the time was the legislative liaison for the Roman Catholic Church to the South African government. He talked about the terrible years of apartheid in South Africa. And he told me about a recent chilling experience. He had been working late at the legislature one night, and the lot where he parked his car was already locked. One of the guards from the legislature offered to drive him home. As they began to make their way, Father Pearson offered directions, but the guard told him, "You don't need to do that. Back in the eighties I was assigned to the team that had you under surveillance. I know where you live."

Father Pearson paused and said to me, "These people did terrible things to us, and they just walked away." His words burned with intensity. And then, after another long pause, he said, with wonder in his voice, "But here we are, over twenty years later, and blood did not run thick through the streets. If we had not been so graceful and forgiving . . . ," and his voice trailed off.

In both Rev. Villa-Vicencio and Father Pearson, I found encouragement to riff on our work and see what new melodies developed, constantly looking for, and trusting, the miraculous solution. When someone comes by our church looking for help in paying a bill and walks out knowing people who want to invest in what she does and can do, a miracle has happened. Do we recognize that there is brokenness, sin, and evil around us? Absolutely. In low-income city neighborhoods, you can't pretend that everything is all right. But we don't let that dissuade us from investing in and building upon and expecting the best of our neighbors.

This trip to South Africa also led to De'Amon's receiving an invitation to spend a month at a Presbyterian church in Gugulethu, one of the townships outside Cape Town. The church wanted De'Amon to do some "roving listener" work in their neighborhood. When De'Amon returned home, he brought many lessons back with him. When he and I talked about them, our ideas were like jazz, one riff leading to another, and we were making music that flowed back and forth between us.

Telling one another the stories of our learning journeys inspires us and gets our imaginations riffing off each other. Let me give you just one example. Kayla, a young woman in our congregation, heard De'Amon and me tell several stories about our trips to South Africa. A few weeks later, Kayla found herself riffing on what she'd heard. She had invited a co-worker to join her at a street festival in her neighborhood. They were enjoying the music, the crowd, and the energy when she noticed some young men squaring off against each other, choosing sides in the crowded street. At that moment she turned to her friend and said, "Follow me." Kayla led the two of them as they danced into the crowd and right into the middle of the young men who were about to fight. As they danced, others in the crowd joined them. Soon the anger cooled, and the fledging fight gave birth to a dance. Clearly, our church's South African stories inspired Kayla. And now we share *her* story.

"Vision is the destroyer of essence."

In the 1980s, several people from Broadway and I visited with Gordon Cosby, founding pastor of Church of the Savior in Washington, D.C. The work that Church of the Savior has done in the Adams-Morgan neighborhood in Washington in health care, housing, and education has been a model of church that has often inspired me. We first met him at a speaking engagement, in a room filled with people eager to hear what this man—who had started a movement that builds on the calling and vocation of the people of God in the city—had to say to them about their work. There was a stunned silence after Gordon finished his talk and summed up what he had said in his slow, gravelly Southern drawl. "Vision," he told us, "is the destroyer of essence." He briefly mentioned all the good work they had done in that neighborhood over the years. "But, in the end," he said, "we had forgotten the essence.

We had forgotten Jesus. We built great institutions. We built great programs. But we forgot Jesus." Even this good work had gotten off the beat.

Part of what I admired about this man and his work was his unflinching attention to what was working and what wasn't. Over the years, Gordon had continued to think about his church's presence in that neighborhood and what this particular place meant to them as people of faith and as practical helpers. When we talked with him afterwards, he reminded us to attend to the presence of Jesus in every person we met in our neighborhood.

Returning home from D.C., my friends and I kept talking about how easy it was to build institutions that serve people — but also how easy it was to stop paying attention to the uniqueness and holiness of each life before us (the Jesus in each person's life). Now, every time we worry that we're building something that has blinded us to the gifts of the people we encounter, we repeat Gordon's words, now a mantra for us: "Vision is the destroyer of essence." Have we gotten off-track?

What Gordon's words helped me see was that, too often, I would brainstorm a rough idea into a clear concept, and I would work to implement it—but I often missed the essence of the Spirit at work in the lives of my neighbors.

A year after the trip to Church of the Savior, Broadway worked on changing our summer program. The long-serving director was actively blocking the changes, so in July I made the hard decision to fire him, telling him he could stay through the end of the summer, and then he'd have to go. Understandably, many of the young men in the neighborhood were upset—the director was a man they'd grown up with. Now they wouldn't talk with me anymore. And I was dreading the summer program's closing banquet. What would happen? Would anyone stage a protest? Would people refuse to leave? Would there be disruptions? I found out soon enough.

I was in my study when banquet day came. I saw several young men—men who had grown up in the old summer program—heading toward the church. People were setting up for the banquet downstairs. I watched as the young men entered the building and then imagined them heading down to the community room. *This is going to be a disaster*, I thought to myself. So I stayed in my office, afraid to confront them. I knew there was probably trouble going on downstairs, and still I didn't move. But, after a couple of minutes, I realized that if I didn't go downstairs and address this issue right away, I wouldn't be able to do the job I needed to do now, and, more importantly, I wouldn't be able to *do* my job at all. I would never regain the respect I needed to work in the neighborhood.

I left my office and ventured downstairs. The young men were walking around the tables set up for their families and friends, the tables with trophies and ribbons laid out, and picking things up and moving them to places they shouldn't be—on the stage or on the chairs, even on the floor. The volunteers were in the kitchen cooking dinner, and I knew that the crowd would start coming in about an hour. If the men continued what they were doing, who knew where this would take us?

I spoke to the young men, my voice shaking, asking them to stop what they were doing. I told them that if they wanted to talk, I was willing. I told them I knew they were angry. The response? They didn't speak to me at all. They just left—everybody but one man. He went to the back of the community room and sat on one of the pews against the wall. When I walked over and sat next to him, I asked his name.

He just looked straight ahead and didn't say a word to me. So I began babbling. I started talking about whatever came to mind. As I talked, I saw the children coming in with their violin cases, heading to the back room to prepare for the opening of the banquet.

I was worried that he was going to cause a scene. Would he yell? Would he try to take over the microphone and spew his anger and hostility toward me at the gathered crowd? I didn't know. So I kept babbling.

Families began to trickle in, and my anxiety level was going up. At that time my wife and I had just discovered she was pregnant with our first child, so I blurted that out. And for the first time the man next to me spoke. He didn't look at me. He just said, "I have a son."

When I asked what his name was, he said, "Trevor."

"Is Trevor seven years old?" I asked as I reached for my wallet. "Yes" was all he said. I pulled out a photo of Trevor's school picture. He had given it to me at the end of the school year, during a conversation we had.

Finally the man loosened up and introduced himself to me as "French." He said he worked for Amtrak and was on the road a lot. We talked about Trevor and the things his son loved. I talked about my worries about becoming a father. When I asked him if he worried as a father, he told me he did.

Then he said, "I don't want Trevor and these kids to make the same mistakes I did." He waved his hand at the gathering throng in the community room, then told me about his battle with addiction and his recent stint in rehab. I asked him how he thought young people could learn from his mistakes. He said he could talk with them and tell them what he knew.

He thought maybe he could teach some classes—at the church, if that would be all right. I said I thought it would be, and I asked him if there were others he knew who would be interested in teaching, too. He thought so.

By now the room was full, and things were about to begin. I was still worried that when the program started, French would forget our conversation and get angry again. So I asked him if he would go to the office with me and help me type up an invitation to a meeting with his friends (many of them were the earlier disrupters), so we could see if his idea would come to life.

As we sat at the computer together, I asked him what he wanted to call the proposed classes. He suggested "The People's Academy." I thought that was the perfect name. When we finished the description, he took what we had typed up and went to show his friends and invite them to be a part of it.

The awards ceremony went on without disruption. The next day French and his friends got together to talk about The People's Academy. Toke was there, and so were Roddrick, Greg, Fat Mike, and Cool Breeze. All were young men who had dropped out of high school. And all had been angry about the firing. But now they wanted to talk about The People's Academy. They talked about what each of them thought they could teach. One of them described how much he loved math. Others talked about writing. Another man showed photos of his art work. They began to make plans.

I invited a teacher who lived in the neighborhood to meet with the young men and assist them in making their dream come to life. They got together the next day, and she began helping them organize this school, this academy, they were creating. She asked them why they wanted to do it. Toke said, "I want my little sister to walk down the street and point at me and say, 'That's my teacher.'" His comment stunned me. I didn't realize this was in his head and in his heart. I remember thinking, *You already are her teacher. The question is, What is your sister already learning from you?*

I thought again about Gordon's words: "Vision is the destroyer of essence." In our context, "vision" is often used to name a really cool idea offered by someone outside the neighborhood. Frequently these ideas come from well-meaning staff people who work and serve in another low-income neighborhood. But the gifts of those young men so eager to teach what they knew in their own community were the "essence." They had something to offer and wanted to do it because they cared, even though many of us who were helpers didn't even consider that possibility. They wanted to be teachers. Why not? It was their essence.

All were young men who had dropped out of high school. But now they wanted to talk about The People's Academy. They talked about what each of them thought they could teach. One of them described how much he loved math. Others talked about writing. Another man showed photos of his art work. They began to make plans.

Five People Who Know You and Love You

In the fall of 2014, a learning journey took me to the Family Independence Initiative in Oakland, California. Years before, its founder, Mauricio Lim Miller, ran the largest social service agency in Oakland. About that experience Mauricio said, "When I was running social services, if I didn't present the charity case, I didn't get funded. We competed to present the most in need. And families come to see that the more needy you are, the more eligibility you have. So the system asks them to hide their talent and initiative."* Frustrated, he closed down the agency, and the Family Independence Initiative was born.

When someone comes to ask for help at the Family Independence Initiative (FII), the first thing the organization does is ask them to come back and bring with them four or five people "who know you and love you." The friends and family members use their gifts and connections to build a two-year plan for the person and his or her community to achieve what he or she wants to accomplish: get clean, purchase a home, go back to school.

Once a quarter, the people check in at FII with their plans, and if they share the data on their progress with their projects,

* David Bornstein, "When Families Lead Themselves Out of Poverty," *New York Times*, August 15, 2017.

they get a cash reward. That's all that happens at the check-in: the staff doesn't try to fix whatever problems might be thwarting someone's goals, or even give advice. The organization is adamant that the staff who work with the people to put together the plans cannot help them accomplish their goals—in fact, any staff who try to do so are fired. FII wants to build up and build upon the agency and power people have in their own lives.

Around our place we sometimes said, with embarrassment, "Stop helping people." But hearing these good folks in Oakland saying the same thing and meaning it in the same way we do encouraged us. It also reminded us to keep asking the people who come to us seeking help, "Who loves you, and what do they say about you and the gifts you have to offer this world?"

Soon after my meeting with FII staff, a man came to church to ask for help with his rent. After we talked for a bit, I asked him to bring in four or five of the people in his life who loved him. When he did, we sat together at a round table at the church, and I asked them to tell me about their friend. The first person who spoke up said, "I've known him since he was a little boy, and I love to go fishing with him. He's good at catching fish." His wife said, "I've been married to him for over ten years, and he is faithful and honest, and he knows how to cook fish!" I was catching a theme.

I knew that the coming Sunday, we'd be hearing the story of the feeding of the five thousand. I asked the man if he could get together some of his friends who liked to fish and if they could be cooking fish as people came out of church, surprising them with a fish lunch—and of course we would pay him for his work! He loved the idea. He grabbed a few friends, and that Sunday noon they fed us all with cornbread and fried catfish. We were moving from one key to another, shifting his ability as an "in-house" fish cook to an outside-of-church fish cook (something he had never imagined before!). That day there was another man at worship who knew a lot of restauranteurs in downtown Indianapolis. He took the fish cook's information, and by the end of the week, he'd been hired at a downtown seafood restaurant. He and his friends were the answers to their own question.

Blood Pressure Posse

I thought I was going on these trips to learn what people were doing so that I could pick up good ideas and try them out for myself. But over time my perspective changed. Eventually I told the people traveling with me and those we sent on trips without me, "Don't come back and tell us you want to do what you saw the people you visited doing. Come back and tell us what you're excited about, how the trip inspired you and what it made you think about."

In South Bend, I took young people from our church to New York City every other summer; in Indianapolis, those trips have been less frequent. (I was following in my father's footsteps: in the early and mid-sixties, my father took youth from French Lick, Indiana, to New York City.) The stories we heard always carried a sense of adventure and edginess I liked because they allowed us to step away from the everyday so that we could come back and see our work at home more clearly. The people we met became our guides. They helped us think about issues facing our own community and spurred our imaginations about what was possible, what could come next.

On one trip to New York City, the youth met with Geoffrey Canada, the author of *Fist, Stick, Knife, Gun*, a book about the growth of violence in that city. (We got the audience with Canada because one of our young people took it upon herself to call Canada's office nearly every day for a month. He finally agreed to meet and talk with us about his life, violence, and the good work his organization, the Harlem Children's Zone, was doing.)

Canada held our young people spellbound as he told them about the switchblade he hid from his mother (she wouldn't have allowed him to keep it). He told them about the hours he spent as

> "Don't come back and tell us you want to do what you saw the people you visited doing. Come back and tell us what you're excited about, how the trip inspired you and what it made you think about."

a teenager in front of the mirror, flipping the knife open and shut as quickly as he could. And about the moment it snapped back and cut one of his fingers deeply. He didn't tell his mother, because then she would have known he was hiding a forbidden weapon. So when they had meals together, he kept his left hand under the table—for several years. As he wound the story down, he held up his hand, and we could see that the top third of his middle finger was bent at a ninety-degree angle.

This is why he ran the Harlem Children's Zone. Canada shared his concerns about growing up in a society in which he needed a knife but couldn't tell his mother about it. He wanted to build safe communities where fear didn't have to hide but could be expressed and addressed. He imagined a community where people could grow up knowing their dreams could come true.

During his conversation with us, Canada explained how the laws cracking down on guns used in drug deals actually put guns in the hands of younger people—because they wouldn't face sentences as severe as those given the older bosses (whose guns they were carrying). His explanation made me realize both the power and the unintended consequences of laws meant to protect communities. Soon I began to wonder if there were unintended consequences of the work we were doing.

And there were. In looking for what was wrong, we were missing a lot of what was right, and this was making things worse. It's difficult to get stronger when all you see are weaknesses. So when we got back from the trip, we took a closer look at our neighborhood and noticed that a lot of people worked in health care. On almost every block we found home health care aides, nurses, dieticians, and orderlies. What the church lay leadership and the staff and I talked about was how to use the gifts of these people to benefit their neighbors. One of the health care workers suggested forming "The Blood Pressure Posse." Their job would be to take the blood pressure of their neighbors every month.

Because of our visit with Canada, we thought carefully about the possible unintended consequences of our proposal. We didn't want people to use the Blood Pressure Posse as an excuse to not visit their own doctors. So we asked the healers of the posse to ask the neighbors they visited to share their information with their doctors, and to follow up with the neighbors to make sure those visits happened.

We also thought about the positive, intended consequences of this endeavor, which fortunately did happen. As members of the Blood Pressure Posse took their neighbors' vital signs, conversations began. One member of the posse discovered that a neighbor of hers was pregnant and wasn't getting prenatal care. Another posse member arranged for her neighbor to visit a doctor. Another found out that a diabetic neighbor of his didn't have a refrigerator in which to keep insulin. Because of that, she had developed gangrene in her foot. The posse member connected her with another neighbor less than a block away who had a refrigerator and who kept insulin for her own diabetes. The woman without a refrigerator not only began using her neighbor's refrigerator—she and her husband also became part-time babysitters for the infant twins of the couple who owned the refrigerator.

The visit with Canada had stirred our imaginations. His sharing his own story reminded us of the stories the young people carried, as well as the stories our neighbors carried. When we faced the unintended consequences of focusing on needs and made a change, people got healthier. If we kept paying attention to those stories, they could lead us into the next steps to take.

Over the years we met a variety of interesting, thought-provoking people in New York. We met with a journalist at the *Village Voice* newsmagazine, people at the National Resources Defense Council, members of the United Nations from around the world, actors in Broadway shows, and people from all sorts of congregations. I was learning that people in congregations, lawyers in offices, journalists at newspapers, parents in their homes—all had power. It was always there, but I hadn't noticed it. People's gifts were hidden to me just as surely as Canada's damaged finger was hidden from his mother. Our conversations not only built community among the people on the trips but gave us a broader view of the world. When we brought our hands out into the open, we could move forward more honestly and realistically. We could see what was there all along but had been hidden either out of shame or out of habit. Our New York trips expanded our repertoire, and opened our eyes to the gifts at home.

"You really want a nun?"

Jazz often involves a good deal of improvisation. Musicians know the chords and the direction of the piece, and begin to experiment with the notes and rhythms of their bandmates. Players who know what they're doing create a new and unique piece on a familiar foundation. They can give new life and breadth to a standard. That happened to me when I took a trip to the Middle East.

In 1993 my wife, Kathy, and I went to Israel and Palestine with a church group. I had read a book called *Blood Brothers* by Elias Chacour. At that time he was a Catholic priest in the town of Ibillin, outside of Nazareth in Galilee. (He's now the bishop for Galilee.)

Reading his book spurred my imagination as a pastor. Chacour wrote so well of the tensions of parish life, the antagonisms in that part of the world, and his striving to bring peace in the midst of

> Muslims, Jews, and Christians all going to school
> side-by-side is a very unusual experience in Israel.
> (Only one percent of the children in that country
> have this opportunity.) "How do you do this?" I
> asked him. "How do you keep people not only go-
> ing to school together, but doing so in peace?"
>
> He answered, "Here we teach people how to be
> human."

these problems. One day Kathy and I rented a taxi and drove out to see Father Chacour. During the visit we saw the school he and others had worked to build there in Ibillin. He explained that they had had to build the school at night because they couldn't get building permits from the government. Muslims, Jews, and Christians all going to school side-by-side is a very unusual experience in Israel. (Only one percent of the children in that country have this opportunity.) "How do you do this?" I asked him. "How do you keep people not only going to school together, but doing so in peace?"

He answered, "Here we teach people how to be human."

As Father Chacour and I talked, he mentioned the nuns who worked with him in his parish, who weren't from his tradition. He's Melkite (Greek) Catholic, and they're Roman Catholic. After he recruited them, the sisters began by visiting the people of his parish. In the process they met a child who was seriously ill, and they sat with the parents and held the child and sang to her. For this and other acts of care, they became known for their healing presence. In a community deeply divided by religion, the sisters brought people together and offered reconciliation where there had been only hostility.

Several years later I was talking with my friend Sister Joy, head of the Holy Cross Order of nuns in our city, whom I had met through some mutual friends in my congregation. I was thinking about Ibillin, and about reaching out across traditions, and I told her that I'd like to have a nun come work with us at Broadway. "Sure you would," she smiled.

A few months later I ran into Sister Joy again, and I said, "I haven't heard from you about my idea of having a nun work with us at the church."

"Were you serious?" she asked.

"Absolutely," I answered. A few weeks later I received a call from Sister Suzanne, who asked if she could come talk with me. When we met, she told me that Sister Joy had sent her my way. She had recently served in Latin America (as an "Animadora"—an Animator!) and was looking for a way to make a contribution back home.

I showed her around. We didn't have money to offer. What we had was amazing neighbors: artists who painted murals telling their stories, chefs who served gourmet meals out of their kitchens, and healers who took their neighbors' blood pressure. Could she help us build on these gifts? I asked her not to give me an answer right away but to think and pray about it.

A month later Sister Suzanne called. "I thought about it, I prayed about it, and then I had a dream," she told me. "I dreamed that I was giving birth, and I took that as a good sign. I want to come work at your church."

We began by introducing Sister Suzanne to some of our neighbors. Two of the people she met ran an "off-the-grid" restaurant out of their home. She visited the woman whose yard bloomed with corn and sunflowers, and who struggled with mental illness. She met a woman who made beautiful quilts but also had no running water in her home. And she found other ways to meet the neighbors. She would attend worship and then hang out at the lunch hosted by the church every Sunday, getting to know the people around each table. She discovered a woman from our neighborhood who made jewelry and connected her with others who were interested in acquiring or selling jewelry. Sister Suzanne moved easily in the rhythm of our neighborhood. Her fluent Spanish and her comfort with living on the margins made her right at home here. She became another engineer building bridges between neighbors and the congregation.

Father Chacour's asking the sisters for help had inspired me. He had noticed where the abundance was, even in surprising places. And while a Roman Catholic sister working in a United Methodist Church isn't common (I don't know of another instance), I was again paying attention to something that had been right in front of me all along (the Catholic nuns near the University of Notre Dame!). It can be hard for me to ask for help, but I'm thankful I did.

A Learning Congregation

My first year in college, an economics professor told me that some "old guys" at his church gathered to play jazz every Thursday night. It was a very informal group. There were no membership fees, no sign-ups, and no grades. You just brought your axe (your instrument) and joined in the music. Sometimes they had sheet music, but most of the time they didn't. It was a blast.

These "old guys" would become my friends, and they later helped my brother get a job when he was trying to figure out what to do next. They also made connections for me when I moved from Indiana to New Jersey for graduate school, so I would know somebody in that strange new place.

When I think about it, I realize that my life has been a continuous process of looking for teachers who can help me make sense of the world around me, challenge me about who and how I will be in the world, and invite me to join them in their work and play.

While our church is called a "teaching congregation" (because of the many interns we host), we're really a learning congregation. At each stop along the way, we've adapted to the changing circumstances in the world around us by paying attention to what's going on and talking with people far and wide to gain perspective on what we're seeing.

The learning journeys we have taken, and will take, open our eyes to even more possibilities. We want to be continually learning so that when the teenage young woman down the street tells us about her dream of being a professional photographer, we'll know some people not only in Indianapolis but in other places around the world who will want to talk with her. These connections will gift her with technical advice, job opportunities, and relationships with those who love the same thing that she does—connections that will serve her for her whole life.

I remember when De'Amon and I visited with Abhijit Banerjee, an economics professor at MIT, who co-wrote a book on global economics (*Poor Economics: A Radical Rethinking of the Way to Fight Global Poverty*). He told us about growing up in India, where he said his early problems in school would have ended in disaster if his parents had been factory workers. But because his parents were academics, his teachers said, "Oh, he must not be challenged enough. He's probably bored. Let's pass him along to the next grade." He looked at us intently then and said, "If my parents had been factory workers, my teachers wouldn't have said that, and I wouldn't have ended up as an economics professor at MIT."

His comment made me think about all the work I had done with young people and how little attention I had paid to their families, their parents. I considered paying more attention to the gifts of the parents, as this professor's teachers had, and not limiting the possibilities for any young person. When I returned from this trip, a group of us asked ourselves how we could see the parents for who they were in their unique blessedness. Out of that question came a new endeavor (well, a new endeavor modeled on a practice we'd already tried out at other seasons in our church life): we now required the youth we hired as summertime "roving listeners" to begin their work by holding a meal that their parents, family members, and friends attended. At the meal we asked the parents to celebrate their son or daughter by telling everyone the goodness they saw in their child. As they did, two things happened. You could see the young person, either shyly or boldly, welcome the words from his or her parents. And the others present began to see the parents for who they were and what they contributed.

At these meals, we've learned about simple gifts and delights. One time, we learned about one young woman who could fix anything broken in her family's house. Another time, the boyfriend (a chef) of the young person's mother told us how much the young man loved to spend time in the kitchen cooking. We've also learned about deep pain and boldness—for example, about the daily humiliations and pain these parents and children experienced as African-Americans and the courage they drew on to deal with indignities and injustice.

One story in particular stays with me. A mother recounted how her son was confronted in a store (she was with him) for having stolen something. She feared that he would be taken downtown and arrested, though she knew he hadn't stolen anything. She started her son's defense by showing the cashier and the owner his empty pockets. They didn't believe her. So in the middle of the store—in order to keep him alive, she thought—she pulled down his pants so the store owner could see he wasn't hiding anything. Those of us who were present at that meal saw the bravery, the decisiveness, and the nimbleness it takes to live in this world. Because of this mother's willingness to share her family's story, we introduced her to another mother we knew had faced similar challenges, so they could support and encourage one another.

Her story also helped us understand her son better and gave us ways to think about his ability to survive and to support other young people struggling with similar grotesque challenges of living in our society.

How would we have known any of these things without the story-telling communities?

Dr. Martin Luther King Jr. said, "In a real sense all life is inter-related. All . . . are caught in an inescapable network of mutuality, tied in a single garment of destiny." My congregation and I have discovered the truth of this in our learning journeys. The teachers we've met along the way have changed us—and made us realize that our congregation needs teachers, as do the young people we work with and their families. These learning journeys have opened our eyes not only to recognize our connections with people a long way from home, but also to become more aware of the people close at hand. In a significant way, the learning journeys to far-flung places have equipped me to see a meal down the block as an equally important learning journey.

A learning person, a learning community, and a learning congregation have given me and the people of our parish a chance to explore what's really going on, to see our communities and their people more fully. Along the way, it became clear to us that the structures and practices we had in place kept us from seeing a lot that was already there. If we were going to treat our neighbors as gifted, imaginative people we couldn't do without, we would have to develop new structures and practices to pay attention to and build on those gifts.

Those "old guys" jamming at the church not only taught me new music and how to play it; they also became my friends. That has happened often through these learning journeys: new relationships have been built that not only teach but also add meaning and depth to my personal life and to my life in my parish.

Keep Playing

Over the years, I've played my trumpet less. Now I listen to jazz on records or on my computer. It's not the same as playing the music, but it does take me back to those moments of playing with the other folks in the band, developing a rapport and a feel for the music, and enjoying the audiences that made the music a little different each time we played it. It felt like magic, like grace, like wonder.

The learning journeys that my friends and I have taken often reminded us of what is in our hands and in our history. Looking into the lives of others helps us see our own lives more clearly. What has really shaped us? What can we learn about our lives and work because of that? When I met with the novelist David James Duncan, he told me a story about how, as a child dealing with the death of his brother, he received his calling to be a writer. When I met with the banker Daryl Collins, she told me a story about how, to get away from people who reminded her of her father, she left her cushy job on Wall Street to become a teacher in Africa.

The conversations have always led us to unexpected places. Hearing the story of a visit with a clergyperson in South Africa opened parishioners' eyes to the possibility of peace, of dancing in the streets of Indianapolis. A visit with a preacher in Washington, D.C., reminded me to never forget the essence in the pursuit of a vision. A visit to a social reformer in New York City inspired us to see those around us with gifts as healers and invest in them as a posse caring for their neighbors. These encounters have taught me, inspired us, and led us into new adventures.

We make progress when people—whether in an office, a classroom, or a bar; on a street corner or a stoop, or around a dining room table—exchange ideas, challenge one another, share experience and wisdom, ask questions, riff off each other's answers, and suggest solutions. Conversation is what utimately led to people walking on the moon, building the first skyscraper, and curing polio. Wonder and magic—we Christians often call it grace—falls on us through our encounters. Around the church we keep on playing, keep on learning, always expanding the circle of people we learn from and journey alongside. The beat never ends.

8

The Lights of Broadway

When you can see abundance where no one expects it, then you begin to see it everywhere. Though it's counter-intuitive, abundance is clearest in communities that are labeled poor and needy—in young people who are called "at-risk" or juvenile delinquents, in old people who are looked at as useless and worn out. Why? Because when all the materialism and pretense of the world are stripped away, what's left is the true picture of a person, who that person is, and what gifts that person brings.

Miss Rose Strides into the Future

"Hello, Reverend." Miss Rose nods to me as I walk past her in our inner-city neighborhood. Every day Miss Rose is out in her housecoat and tennis shoes sweeping the street, picking up trash.

Her dusky gray complexion fits in well on this block. It blends with the pink of her worn robe and the salt-and-pepper gray of the sidewalk. She's seen it all and then some. She's known blood to run in the gutters. She's heard the shouts, then shots, so common that they're often unnoticed. She's tall. The years have not bent her . . . much. Perhaps it's all that walking, that striding into the future.

The years have not bent her . . . much. Perhaps it's all that walking, that striding into the future.

She has cared for her children, her grandchildren, and her great-grandchildren. Now in her eighties, she continues the work of building community. Piece by piece she picks up lives often left behind and finds a place for them in her home, in her community—the glorious in the gritty.

She has cared for her children, her grandchildren, and her great-grandchildren. Now in her eighties, she continues the work of building community. Piece by piece she picks up lives often left behind and finds a place for them in her home, in her community—the glorious in the gritty.

She watches from her porch. Sunflowers in her front yard, beans in the back yard—she knows how to grow things. Out front, broken pavement lies open to the brick from generations ago. Fences line yards to the left and to the right, barriers against violence but also against friendship.

Day after day, Miss Rose steps into the street. She looks both ways. Empty patchwork lots and old homes fill the block. Children, families, and papers swirl around her. The Spirit blows and the papers dance, sometimes out of her reach. She watches; she knows where the Spirit's blowing. Every once in a while she reaches down and picks up a piece of paper. Here is the slow, steadfast work of building community on broken pavement. Crushed cans and shattered glass are part of her collection. She gathers up the broken and damaged and creates something beautiful.

Kids play curb ball as she cleans the street. Young people walk by as she picks up trash. They notice but don't say anything. They walk with the easy, unknowing confidence of the young. They see and don't see. Their feet land heavy. Hers glide. They laugh and talk loud. She smiles and says little. Others—television reporters, teachers, preachers, even neighbors—tell them how bad their neighborhood is.

Daily, Miss Rose cleans the street. She does her part, quietly inviting others to do theirs.

Joe King Talks to the Creek

Joe King takes over the room as soon as he walks in. Plaid shirt and blue jeans—he wears them like a suit. He's at home in the boardroom or the woods. He's all energy and explosions—laughter, ideas, movement. Always.

For years until he retired he sold insurance, writing policies, keeping his neighbors safe and healthy. He loves a good time. The best is fishing with friends and telling each other stories.

Joe is always close to the water. It's a member of his community. Fall Creek is never very wide, no more than forty-five to fifty yards. During the dry summer months, it can slow to a trickle. In the spring and in the fall, it flows with more vigor, carrying fish but also garbage.

Fall Creek isn't the strong Wabash, isn't the mighty Mississippi, but these waters have fed people. As a boy, fatherless, Joe would wade into the waters of Fall Creek, where the men would gather and fish. These men became his fathers, his teachers. They taught him about fish, about life in the city—about life.

We go down by the waters, Joe and I. Every day he steps into Fall Creek. Even now, he leads a clean-up of Fall Creek twice a year. Why? "Because," he says, "I talk to the creek, and the creek talks to me, and I tell it I will not forsake it."

His whole life he has loved this water. It's more than H_2O to him. The water cleanses and heals. It breathes, frees, reveals, teaches. It has been his school, his home, his grocery store, his bank. As the men fished, they caught him. Instead of ignoring him or using him, they fed him. Every day he is grateful for the ways the waters have gathered and nourished community.

Joe and his friends—neighbors young and old, women and men—gather to feed each other by the waters of Fall Creek. Their relationship to it reminds me of the words of John in the book of Revelation:

> Then the angel showed me the river of the water of life, bright as crystal, flowing from the throne of God and of the Lamb from the middle of the street of the city. On either side of the river is the tree of life with its twelve kinds of fruit, producing its fruit each month; and the leaves of the tree are for the healing of the nations. Nothing accursed will be found there. (Rev. 22:1–3)

"Nothing accursed will be found there." Joe sees his community that way. He has helped me see our neighborhood, its citizens, and the nature surrounding us with the eyes of faith. "Nothing accursed will be found there." Nothing indeed.

Unexplored Territories

The stories of Miss Rose and Joe King are at the same time unique and representative. Their lives are visible to us, and we are able to build and act on the goodness in them. But the systems and structures in our church, government, social service organizations, and our society as a whole often work against our efforts to pay attention to the other souls in our small patches of the earth.

Many years ago, I, along with other people from churches around the country, attended a conference called "Engaging in Ministry with the Poor." When asked to describe what the church could and should be doing in low-income neighborhoods, most of my interlocutors at the conference talked about excellent faith-based community organizing efforts like those led by the Direct Action & Research Training Center (DART), People Improving Communities through Organizing (PICO), and Gamaliel. Those groups assist congregations and other institutions that work with and serve low-income neighborhoods and people. But congregations aren't the same as citizens. I asked what efforts congregations could be involved in that were citizen-centered rather than institution-centered. The room got quiet.

"None," the experienced leader said.

What does a citizen-centered effort look like? At the time, I didn't know. But my neighbors, including Miss Rose and Joe King, have taught me. The principles and practices our congregation is developing prepare us to recognize the giftedness of those around us. "Poverty," Sam Wells says in *A Nazareth Manifesto*, is "a mask we put on people to hide their true wealth."*

When we insist on looking behind that mask, we do indeed find untold wealth. The woman who came to the church looking for a way to keep the water flowing in her pipes was also a good mother and an excellent cook. The man signing up his son for the tutoring program was a talented musician. The mother who wanted her daughters to learn to play the violin in the summer program knew a lot about building community with her neighbors. The methamphetamine addict made an excellent chairperson of our finance committee. The woman who lived with bipolar disorder for over twenty years was a discerning chairperson of our governing council.

And once your community discovers such wealth, you want to share it.

---

* Samuel Wells, *A Nazareth Manifesto: Being with God* (Hoboken, NJ: Wiley, 2015), 116.

> The principles and practices our congregation is developing prepare us to recognize the giftedness of those around us. "Poverty," Sam Wells says in *A Nazareth Manifesto*, is "a mask we put on people to hide their true wealth."

Sharing the Wealth

After two years as our roving listener, De'Amon felt he was spending too much time in the neighborhood. He wasn't "roving" outside of his community. He wanted to get out and share the wealth. There were lots of gifts in this neighborhood and its people that were unseen, and he wanted to connect those gifts with the larger world. He was right. But he didn't know how to do it.

So the personnel committee of the church had a conversation with De'Amon and asked him to spend one night a week at a local bar outside of the immediate neighborhood. His responsibility was to tell other patrons three stories of people in our neighborhood and to bring back three stories of people he met in the bar.

One of these evenings, De'Amon met a physician who invited him to speak to his Sunday school class at a large suburban church. A few weeks after that event, a woman from that church who works for the child and maternal health division of the Indiana Department of Health called our church and asked, "Could your staff meet with our staff this afternoon?"

When the Department of Health requests an immediate meeting, you worry about it a little. I asked, "Why do you want to meet with us?"

"We'll tell you when we get there," she replied.

At the meeting, the woman from the state began by saying, "Our job is to make the people of this state healthier, and we haven't been doing that well. We believe what you're doing is actually making communities healthier. We have a grant to make communities healthier, and we'd like to give it to you to build on your work."

What makes communities healthier, stronger, and better? Growing the gifts of people who care about their neighbors, who visit each other when they're sick and offer healing, who throw good parties to celebrate life and joy, who are talented carpenters, cooks, gardeners, administrators, organizers, and artists.

In our practices we paid attention to the musicians and entrepreneurs and joined them in their adventures. We listened as parents taught their children and young people explored their imaginations and old folks wrote poetry about life on the streets outside their doors. We did this in order to discern our next steps. We had shifted our planning from "Here's what we're going to do" to "Here's how and what we're going to learn."

The Department of Health invested $250,000 in our neighbors. We used the money to grow the listening work the young people were doing during the summer: we hired more young people and increased their hours. At summer's end, a local university evaluated the work.

Over the course of the summer, the "rovers" (the young people who were doing the naming, blessing, and connecting work) selected sixty of their neighbors to come together for a two-day conversation. We paid the neighbors for their time. In the room where Broadway members had once collected toys and underwear to hand out to poor children, neighbors now gathered to talk about their individual experiences of pregnancy, parenting, marriage, and more. Poet and neighbor Mari Evans keynoted the event. She spoke about the deaths of her two adult sons over the previous five years. One son developed cancer in his sixties, and months before he died, during a period when she spent significant time with him, she learned he'd been sexually abused by a female relative of theirs from the time he was nine until he was twelve. She told the crowd, "I wish I had known of this abuse well before those last six months. It explained a lot of issues in his life. I always thought of myself as a mother who was on top of things. . . . We need to pay attention to our children." She spoke these truths in a calm voice free of melodrama. And her willingness to share her story so authentically set the tone for the coming conversations of those who had gathered.

Neighbors discussed finances, abortion, parenting, and more. People listened to one another, laughed, cried, and got angry, but mainly they shared stories from their lives. An older woman talked about the experience of an abortion she had undergone years ago. She said, "Sometimes at night I hear the distinctive sound of the machine they used in the procedure." A woman near her looked at her, eyes wide, and whispered, "You, too?" Both recognized the shame and stigma associated with abortion in our culture, and that stigma had kept both of them from talking to other women about their experiences.

As people shared their stories, they were set free to reveal and act on what they cared most deeply about. They met each other where their lives intersected, and in those places of intersection, they found community and kinship. And a sense of identification and intimacy grew as people recognized each other as sisters and brothers in that gathering.

Representatives from institutions that provide child and maternal health services attended our gathering. They found their roles flipped upside down—the wisdom about health and family structure was coming not from them, but from the people they usually helped. Young people were talking about safe sex; older women were talking about pregnancy and how they had taken care of themselves. Men were talking about what it meant to them to be fathers.

Staff from the neighborhood development corporation met people they had never talked with before. They listened as neighbors dreamed of empty lots full of children and art. Other neighbors told stories of the parties, meals, and music that filled their lives.

Out of this gathering came other powerful connections, both anticipated and unexpected. The researchers had planned to hear people talk about things they wanted to see happen. What they didn't expect was that the neighbors would develop and implement an action plan. Young women and older women talked about intentionally spending time together to learn from each other. These neighbor women ended up starting "Prestigious Princesses," which brings young women and older women together on a regular basis throughout the school year. At an annual banquet, each young woman shares with her neighbors and family her dreams for her life as well as what she has learned and accomplished that year. Outside the organization, these women also see each other socially, building connections between their families and making the neighborhood a healthier, less violent place. These connections developed not from a strategic plan made by an outside organization, but from neighbors talking with one another and building on what they were already doing.

The gathering allowed other good things to bubble up—neighbors letting others know about jobs available or sharing their art with each other. None of these ideas came from the church. Yes, we played a role. We provided space for people to meet each other and talk with each other. And the church was the conduit for the grant money.

But it was the gathering itself that reminded people of the goodness present in a place where we too often see only needs and problems. It was a celebration of community that built stronger social networks within the neighborhood and built partnerships with institutions and agencies looking for what was wrong, not what was right. Ditching the strategic plan, we strategically listened to what was being said and what was waiting to be born. That's how both individuals and communities get stronger and healthier.

Six Principles

Six years ago, I was speaking to the local neighborhood development corporation. One of the leaders asked me how the church would articulate the principles that guide us in our work. I, in turn, posed that question to the leaders of the congregation, and we came back with these six principles that named why we do what we do and what we expect from others.

1. *Our neighbors are God's people. Act like it.*

We believe all people are beloved children of God, so we expect institutions that serve them to treat them accordingly. Institutions largely ignore the people of the neighborhood as anything other than recipients of their service, viewing them as people to be fixed, people in need, people who are empty. While this perspective may not reflect their feelings about people, it captures their practice.

We used to do needs surveys in the congregation. On Pentecost in 1992, we started asking different questions, and Adele and her excellent cooking ushered us through the doorway. Asking people not what they needed or what they lacked, but what they loved, cared about, and acted on in their lives sent us to the neighborhood looking to mine the treasures there.

Organizations we partner with could do the same thing. If they provide a service, they could ask the people they serve, "Who loves you, and what do the people who love you say is the best thing about you?" They could ask, "What three things could you teach that you already know?" (But they should ask that only if they're going to try to do something concrete with the answer.) In other words, they could treat people with respect and greet them with loving curiosity. Helping organizations aren't going to stop providing their services, but they can treat the recipients as if they have something valuable to offer to the world and to their community.

2. *Everything begins with and builds on the gifts of our neighbors.*

We are committed to identifying the gifts, capacities, talents, dreams, and passions that people have, and to investing in them. We expect institutions to acknowledge the gifts of the people they "serve," and to find some way to utilize those gifts. If the people who are being served are the first people involved in the effort, then it has a good chance of being something that those being served really want (and then might use!). One phrase that reminds us to begin with the people we serve is "Nothing about me, without me."

In 2004, Broadway decided that if any new service was going to be provided by the congregation, people who were being served must be part of the leadership team for that service. This guideline kept us from developing programs in which no one was really interested.

I had ignored this rule for many years and, without any input from the people I was hoping to help, had offered budgeting classes, parenting classes, and exercise groups. Sometimes there was a burst of energy at the beginning, but the classes didn't continue for long. By contrast, when we invested in what our neighbors were already doing, as in the School of the Spirit, we discovered there was a long-term constituency for that activity, and we didn't have to do the recruiting.

While investing in what people were already doing wasn't a complex idea, making room for their enterprises by giving up our own pet projects was challenging. Building on the gifts of our neighbors took time and intention. We encouraged our partners not to bite off more than they could chew, to start small—to find the easiest, most evident gift to build from and see what happened. Then we could celebrate it and tell others about it.

3. Parents and guardians are the first and best teachers. Respect this.

Because we know any child's parents and guardians are his or her first and best teachers, we do all we can to show children that we see and acknowledge the value, primacy, and gifts of these significant people in their lives. So when we work with children, we talk with the parents and guardians, learning about them and who they are, and at least informing them about an activity before involving the children in it.

For many years, when I ran youth groups and programs, I was guilty of involving young people and often never meeting their parents. Of course, I met some, but that was because the parents made the effort (and often it took significant effort, as I was constantly on the move). Even when I met the parents, I never turned to them as resources who could help me or their sons and daughters.

The connection that I forged with French because I knew his son Trevor taught me a great lesson about the power parents have, especially in low-income communities. They care deeply and passionately for their children, and they want things to be better for them.

Organizations and institutions serving youth can begin their work by paying attention to one parent and building on something that parent has to offer. They can ask the parent to tell them what they see and notice about their children. They can ask the children to tell them the best things they can think of about their parent(s). Gathering this information and then celebrating it with the whole group or agency, and then publicizing these words and affirmations, can help open everyone's eyes to what is so often missed.

4. We invest first and foremost in the good the people of the neighborhood seek.

Doing things *for* people and involving neighbors in what "we" (as institutions) do hasn't been effective. At our church, we experiment with ways to invest in the good things our neighbors are doing before we ask them to be involved in what we're doing. The church asks other institutions to think about this as well—first asking not "How can we involve people?" but "How can we be involved with people?" Asking the right question can lead us to new awareness of the power that is present and active in our communities. Institutional leaders who have often felt lonely and isolated in their work can find themselves invigorated as they grow more aware of the abundance around them.

Schools, churches, and social service agencies will benefit their organizations as well as the people they serve to the extent that they invest in the giftedness of the people around them. Such investment builds up people's sense of agency, an awareness of power that people on the margins often don't feel. When people discover or are reminded of their agency, the programs they're involved with will take truly amazing turns. Broadway knows this firsthand. When a teenager and his friends dressed up like Santa Claus and delivered presents to their neighbors on Christmas Eve, relationships were mended and built. When another neighbor tutored the children on her block and involved their families in her good work, other neighbors began to take notice and wanted to support it.

Organizations and institutions need to remember that often they came into being because a few committed, gifted, passionate people came together around something they deeply cared about and created these formal groups. Encouraging those organizations to allow others to do the same can help them rediscover their roots and their passion.

5. *Money must flow to the neighborhood.*

Our neighborhood is low-income, which means we don't have a lot of money. So if money is available, most if not all of it should end up in the hands of people who live in the neighborhood.

The flow of money can be a difficult subject for individuals, associations, and organizations working with low-income and other marginalized peoples. Fighting the paternalism that comes from controlling the purse strings is difficult. But that fight is worthwhile, because institutions can help to grow the power of the community by bringing money to and keeping money in the community.

I remember the first time that leaders at our church told an informal association of neighbors who had been offered money by a local family foundation that we would receive the money the foundation was offering them (they needed to file a 501(c) 3 to receive funds) and that we wouldn't keep one penny for ourselves. We also made it clear that we weren't going to do the project, only support their doing the project. The role wasn't one we had played or even considered before. We did it because a neighbor asked us to, and after talking it over and praying about it, we decided to say yes. When other agencies, such as the state health department, wanted to support our work with our neighbors, they were very surprised when we explained that we wouldn't take the money for ourselves, but that we wanted to think with them about how this money could end up in the hands of our neighbors.

Many institutions can't imagine putting money into the hands of the people they serve—in part because institutions don't always trust these people, and in part because all institutions could use even small amounts of money to support the administration of their organizations. But at Broadway, we've found that when we equipped our neighbors with money, we got a substantial return, because investing in our neighbors helped encourage more and more of them who were doing good work. We noticed the increase in our neighbors' energy and public activity.

> Many institutions can't imagine putting money
> into the hands of the people they serve—in part
> because institutions don't always trust these
> people, and in part because all institutions could
> use even small amounts of money to support the
> administration of their organizations. But at
> Broadway, we've found that when we equipped
> our neighbors with money, we got a substantial
> return, because investing in our neighbors helped
> encourage more and more of them who were doing
> good work. We noticed the increase in our neigh-
> bors' energy and public activity.

Institutions and associations can direct funding into the hands of people who don't have a lot. In our case, doing so hasn't cost more; it's simply required redirecting the funding we already had. In the old summer program, we took the money and paid people outside our neighborhood to run programming for young people from our neighborhood. In what we do now, the money goes to young people who live in our neighborhood. We used to pay people outside our neighborhood to cater meals. Now people inside our neighborhood do that work. And because they cater meals at the church, they often get hired by people who have attended these meals.

Our process hasn't hurt our bottom line for two reasons. First, when things are better for our neighbors, they're better for everyone. And second, our actions have caught the attention of other organizations that wanted to think with us about the issue we were working on. Those organizations have often returned to us with ideas for investing in our neighbors, and sometimes those organizations have invested money—like the hospital that put $40,000 into the hands of gardeners in our neighborhood.

6. Practice neighbor love.

Practice hospitality. We ask our partners—institutions both inside and outside our neighborhood that want to work with us—to treat each other as neighbors. It's easy to talk with each other like you would talk with someone at your dinner table. In fact, we encourage our partners to share meals together as often as possible.

At the center of neighbor love is curiosity—about the world and about other people. Around the church, we call this mutual delight. We also call it discovery. The novelist and theologian Sara Maitland says that we all need "jewel detectors,"* and pastor and writer Donna Schaper calls us to be "detectives on the track of the holy."*

When we're in love with someone, we're in a constant process of discovery and learning. Together we're growing something powerful and life-changing. That happens regularly around a dinner table and hardly ever around a conference table.

When we first hired the young people to be roving listeners during the summer, we simply put them to work. Now, as I mentioned earlier, before their work begins, the church hosts meals with their families and friends, and people tell them what they know and see in the lives of those young people. We used to visit shut-ins in their homes. Now, instead of having an individual make a solo visit to the shut-in person, we gather people for a meal with the shut-in: family and friends come and tell the person what blessings he or she has given their lives.

In these gatherings we practice a great deal of intention. We don't just serve a good meal. We create a chance to discover more about one another, a chance to deepen our love for one another. Every time I've attended one of these meals, something has happened that I didn't expect. Whether two people discovered their

---

* Sara Maitland, *A Joyful Theology* (Minneapolis: Augsburg, 2002), 124.
* Donna Schaper, *A Book of Common Power: Narratives Against the Current* (San Diego: Luramedia, 1989), 97.

> At the center of neighbor love is curiosity—about
> the world and about other people. Around the
> church, we call this mutual delight. We also call
> it discovery. The novelist and theologian Sara
> Maitland says that we all need "jewel detectors,"
> and pastor and writer Donna Schaper calls us to
> be "detectives on the track of the holy."

common love of opera or a grandfather told his granddaughter about an important part of their heritage, we have heard stories that have brought people growth and maturity.

When we got out of our building and opened ourselves up to receive hospitality as well as to share it, the learning and discovery expanded. Organizations and institutions can find ways, maybe just a few times a year, to put their people in the homes of the neighbors they serve. If, in gathering together, people *intend* to listen and to learn from one another—not about some issue, but about each other's lives and gifts—then new doors will appear and open.

There are good questions to ask at those times. *How did your passion—this love of art, music, mathematics, literature, business— develop? What would the people who know you best say about that?* These questions work for gang-bangers and Wall Street bankers. You can ask people what's on their bucket list and what's the bravest thing they've ever done. The challenge is to pay attention and to follow where the story leads, not just listen for the answer, check it off in your mind, and go on to the next question.

*   *   *

My coworkers, our congregants, and I often talk about these six principles with one another. We consider how they're useful, and we ask if they need any revision. The principles remind us what we need to pay attention to as we live in community with one another. They remind us that people don't live on bread alone.

Gamifying Community

Once we named these principles in our church, we clergy and lay leaders asked ourselves what we could do to both keep in touch with and reinforce the principles. Because these principles challenged our long-standing structures, practices, and habits, we knew they wouldn't come naturally. We noticed, for example, that we treated people who had less money differently from those who had more money.

So our clergy, staff, and lay leaders began experimenting with what's called "gamifying" our work. In the book *Reality Is Broken*, Jane McGonigal argues that games are often very helpful to both learning and making things work. She cites a report from the ancient historian Herodotus about a king who kept the people of his kingdom alive through a long famine by having them play games and fast on one day, and work and eat on the next day. The people of the kingdom followed this practice for eighteen years. If games could be used in this dire circumstance, they could also help us to see abundance where before we saw scarcity—and, ultimately, to change the way we treated people who had less money.

Our denomination, like many, asks us to count how many people attend worship services on Sunday and also to count how much money is collected at those services. The same type of reporting is used in education and other areas of public life. But counting the attendance and the offering wasn't giving us any information we could use. It wasn't helping us see our neighbors more clearly. It wasn't coming close to opening our eyes to the abundance around us.

So our pastors and lay leaders of the congregation talked with one another about what actions we could count that would

127

both reflect what we believe and help us pay attention to and celebrate those actions. We came up with twelve actions or practices that would reinforce the six principles. And we set up our own game that we played every month: whoever scored the most points at the end of the month bought cupcakes for all the other players. These are the scoring opportunities we put together:

1. Count the number of people whose homes you went to, on whom you laid hands and blessed, and for whom you offered a prayer of celebration and praise for their vocation in their life, home, and workplace.
2. Count the number of people you introduced to each other because "I see in each of you the same call and claim of God upon your life, and it seemed like it would be great for you to know that about each other."
3. Count the number of people you prayed with in hospital rooms, on street corners, in alleys, in living rooms, in offices, and in car repair shops.
4. Count the number of people to whom you wrote letters celebrating their discipleship/vocation in the life of the world.
5. Count the number of people you anointed with oil as they prepared for a challenge before them.
6. Count the number of people you journeyed with to visit someone else at home, at the hospital, or in the workplace.
7. Count the number of people you visited to remind them of their baptism (perhaps on an anniversary of their baptism or on the baptismal anniversary of someone in their household).
8. Count the number of times you ate with someone and reminded them during the meal of the communion that Jesus shared with his friends on Maundy Thursday and of Christ's presence at their table.
9. Count the number of times you went and offered forgiveness to someone who was laboring under guilt and shame.

> Count the number of people you prayed with in
> hospital rooms, on street corners, in alleys, in liv-
> ing rooms, in offices, and in car repair shops.

10. Count the number of times you threw a party to celebrate the
    presence and power of God's love in the people and parish
    around you.
11. Count the number of times you took your Bible and read a
    story to someone whose life you see in that particular story.
12. Count the number of times you posted on Facebook celebrat-
    ing in concrete and joyful ways the discipleship/vocation of
    the people in your parish.

By engaging in these practices, we were acting our way into
new ways of thinking. The new practices opened our eyes to things
that had always been there, but that we hadn't been seeing. And
we discovered, in our gamifying, that opportunities to score points
came to us nearly as often as we sought them out.

If we look at the world in new ways and consequently be-
have differently, new opportunities arise. I myself carry a little
container of oil in my pocket so that I can bless people when the
opportunity presents itself. One Good Friday as I was walking in
the neighborhood, a man ran up to me. He said, "Are you from
Broadway?" I told him I was.

He asked, "Would you anoint me with oil?"

"Sure," I replied. "What would you like me to celebrate or pray
for in this anointing?" I asked.

He said, "I want healing from an addiction I'm fighting and a
blessing for me as a father to my two children." On a busy street
in Indianapolis, on a Friday morning, he knelt on the broken
sidewalk, and I anointed him with oil and reminded him of God's
blessing as we prayed.

Institutions and individuals who want to build on the abundance around them need to be able to see that abundance. The game we developed positively reinforced our new way of looking at the world—and we needed that encouragement and focus. Otherwise our attention would have been directed in other places.

Needed: A Willingness to Risk

While talking with me about this book, a friend asked me, "You aren't suggesting that people fly over poor neighborhoods and drop bales of twenty-dollar bills, are you?" While that isn't what I'm suggesting, I think it would be better than 90 percent of what I used to do, and I think it would be more useful than most of the programs provided by social service efforts.

One example here will make my point. About five years ago, a coalition of religious and secular organizations came together in our city to run a program called "Circles out of Poverty." They raised two million dollars for this effort, and during this time they called to ask for our congregation's support. I asked them if they would be open to an experiment. I proposed they give us a million dollars, and we would give ten families in our neighborhood one hundred thousand dollars each. And at the end of two years we would see which one of us had done more to bring people out of poverty. They were unwilling to accept this challenge.

But experiments like that are worth doing. Real change requires the willingness to risk and test. The Circles out of Poverty program closed down after their two-year run in our city, and hardly anyone noticed. The people who made money from the program were the people employed to run it.

Most anti-poverty efforts offer solutions that have been proven not to work. Yet they continue, until they disappear and aren't replaced. Churches close, social service programs run out of money, and people just get tired and quit. Yet our congregations

> Real change requires the willingness to risk and
> test.

and communities are filled with imaginative, innovative, and extraordinary people who can help us discover the answers right in front of us. Many of those gifts are in the hands of the very people whom others are committed to serving.

A New Way of Seeing

At the beginning of this book, I noted that I'm not proposing a model for the work of ministry, for urban ministry, or for any work with low-income neighborhoods or citizens. There is no replicable system to be imitated in community after community: no multiplying of no-poverty simulations, no circles-out-of-poverty programs we can buy online will change communities. Only attention to the wondrous children of God around us and the gifts they bring to the table will make a lasting difference.

What this book does offer is a way of looking at the world, a set of lenses. When Wendell Berry was asked about what kind of economy is the best, he said the best economy is the kingdom of God. That isn't a capitalist economy or a socialist economy. It's an economy where attention is paid to every hair on our head, to the ways in which the flowers of the field are dressed, and to God's abundance in the most surprising places.

It's an economy of attention and intention—an economy, as in our neighborhood, where people who are discounted by the world are seen for the gifts they bring to bear. It's an economy where Miss Rose's care for her yard and cleaning up of the streets are celebrated. It's an economy where, on neighbor Orlando's front porch, music lessons are taken note of and praised. It's an econ-

> When Wendell Berry was asked about what kind
> of economy is the best, he said the best economy is
> the kingdom of God. That isn't a capitalist econ-
> omy or a socialist economy. It's an economy where
> attention is paid to every hair on our head, to the
> ways in which the flowers of the field are dressed,
> and to God's abundance in the most surprising
> places.

omy where neighbor Martha's singing voice rises from the bus stop and blesses the young people returning from school, and the community sings her praises.

Years ago my friend and colleague Philip Amerson dreamed about going to churches around the country and saying, "Pay us half of what you're paying for the latest Miracle-Gro church program you have. We'll spend the next two years reminding the people of the churches of the romance of ministry. Let's see which gets better results." The romance of ministry, the romance of work in low-income communities is to recognize and celebrate the wonder and beauty that are present and growing. The work of life is a science, but it is also an art.

Too often organizations, churches, and others in low-income neighborhoods make commitments based more on the advice of planners than on the movement of the Spirit, on the giftedness all around us. We call in the consultants to "fix us" rather than calling in our bosses or bishops to "bless us."

The file cabinets of organizations in poor neighborhoods are filled with reports arguing that if they could just build a parking lot or invest in advertising or add a new staff person, they would once again thrive. Once those reports are received, they're rarely, if ever, looked at again. And if they are looked at more than once, they inspire only guilt among those who realize they failed to accomplish the goals set for them.

Churches could lead the way in making a real change. What if, in the city, we asked our denominational leaders to come to us, lay hands on us and bless us, and thank us for keeping our commitment to stay in the city when others have fled? What if, at annual church conferences, instead of celebrating only the church that grew by the biggest number or the largest percentage, we celebrated the faithfulness of those congregations? What if we gave awards to congregations that, despite all that has happened around them demographically—all the shifts, the white flight, the changing economic base—have stayed in the city to witness to God's goodness, grace, glory, and gifts in the people of God? What if we asked those congregations to name three neighbors they wanted to celebrate for the gifts they give in that neighborhood?

The issues our organizations and people face cannot be cured by technique (whether that technique is creating a new worship service, erecting a new building, storytelling, or establishing an economic and community development program). But we do have the tools we need in our own hands. They are the tools of our faith—the tools that brought us to the point we are today. Our primary tool is trusting in the present abundance, the tool that so many of us have abandoned as we have grown afraid to die—and afraid to live. I try to remember those words that appear in Scripture so often: "Fear not."

Two Things Became Visible

In 1986, I imagined young people pouring through the doors into the hallways of Broadway to be tutored. They would go into classrooms full of supplies and be met by smiling tutors, who would take them from Cs and Ds to As and Bs. We were staffed with volunteers provided by Broadway and other congregations in the city. We had also recruited volunteers through United Way and from Eli Lilly and Co., a major pharmaceutical company headquartered in Indianapolis.

The existing tutoring program was well established but sloppily run: there wasn't much continuity from week to week; students and volunteers weren't reliably present.

So the church began looking for more volunteers. A young woman from another congregation, a talented educator, put together a curriculum that strengthened what we were doing. We gathered the tutors, and she worked with them to prepare them for working with the students. We provided more than fifty tutors, one-on-one, Tuesday through Thursday.

Broadway Church was working to knock down the walls between volunteers and recipients, but it wasn't easy. Most programs were structured in ways that reinforced those walls. And all the help was coming from the outside.

When I returned to Broadway in 2005, the tutoring program was continuing to hum along. Then one day De'Amon phoned me and told me I should talk with someone he met while roving. "You need to call Maya."

When I asked him why, he answered, "Because she runs a tutoring program out of her home."

"What do you mean?" I asked.

"You just need to talk with her," he said, and after leaving me her number, he hung up. We had never asked for tutors from our neighborhood. Maybe this was the beginning of something new.

When I called Maya, I was thinking, *Maybe she can tutor in our program.* Now in her mid-thirties, she'd lived in the neighborhood her whole life. Both of her parents were dead, and she was living in the house in which they had raised her. I told her I had heard she was running a tutoring program. She explained that she worked at AT&T at night, and that during the summer, on weekdays, she had her young neighbors over to tutor them.

"What do you cover?" I asked.

"Everything from phonics to Sophocles," she told me. "If they don't know how to read, we work on phonics. If they're older, I cover everything I can, including Sophocles. And then on Fridays I have a cookout, and their families come over, and they present their work from the week."

Wow, I thought. *We shouldn't be asking her to tutor. We should be figuring out how we could support her work.* And so we began doing that.

It started simply. One of the lay leaders of our congregation called and asked Maya to attend worship the following Sunday, so we could celebrate her good work. She said she'd be delighted to come. The lay leader also asked another neighbor, whom he knew through De'Amon's roving, to make a cake to celebrate Maya's contribution.

On that Sunday, Maya walked into worship. Still a young woman with a young woman's stride, she was dressed up—hat, gloves, and dress all perfectly matched. The older white women in the front row gave her approving glances. Her soft caramel skin stood out against the dark stain of our pews. It was her first time ever in the building, she told us. She sat in the front row, and when it came time, the lay leader stepped forward and asked her to stand up. She did—with her back to the congregation. He told them about her work (she didn't want to speak from the microphone), and then he said, "If you will support Maya's work with your prayers, your presence, your gifts, your service, and your witness, please stand." Almost everyone in the congregation stood up, but Maya didn't know it because she was in the front row with her back to the standing assembly.

Then the lay leader borrowed from the wedding liturgy of the church and asked, "Will all of you do everything in your power to support and care for this person in her ministry? If so, will you answer, 'We will'?"

And the congregation thundered, "WE WILL!"

And Maya, in her Sunday finest, leapt up in the air and turned around. When she landed, both she and the congregation saw something that had been hidden from our eyes.

We hadn't noticed there were people—neighbors—doing this remarkable work in our neighborhood. And Maya hadn't realized there was a whole congregation of people who were willing to pledge their support in spiritual and practical ways for the work she was doing—her calling. How did we know it was her calling? Because nobody asked her to do it, and she did it anyway. And she did it well. She knew her power, and she acted on it.

From that day forward, people in the congregation offered encouragement and invested in what Maya was doing. Some sent letters thanking her for her good work, and others asked what type of materials she might need and provided them. Some attended the Friday gatherings in which the children and their families came together. As members of the church began to support Maya, they began to see not only her good work, but other good work happen-

> We hadn't noticed there were people—neighbors—doing this remarkable work in our neighborhood. And Maya hadn't realized there was a whole congregation of people who were willing to pledge their support in spiritual and practical ways for the work she was doing—her calling. How did we know it was her calling? Because nobody asked her to do it, and she did it anyway. And she did it well. She knew her power, and she acted on it.

ing on the block. And it began to change what church members told others in their circles about what people in our so-called bad neighborhood were doing.

Standing in the sanctuary that Sunday morning, I was still being schooled. De'Amon had helped me see Maya, and now I knew that the congregation could see her, too. I was learning that we had power as a congregation, as a community, well beyond the tutoring, to welcome, affirm, and bless her good work, her holy calling. Maybe, like the poet Milosz, we could "glorify things just because they are."

Afterword

Today, Broadway Church has two full-time pastors, me and the Rev. Dr. Rachel Metheny, and a part-time volunteer deacon. We also employ a minister of music, a building superintendent, a custodian, an administrative assistant, and an accompanist. Moving in and out of our life together are interns from theological schools and seminaries, from schools of social work, from colleges and from music programs. The congregation itself is a delightfully eclectic mix of people. While many members could walk to Broadway, we are a metropolitan congregation drawing members from across the city. There are many children and youth, young couples and families, and a couple of active members who are over 100 years old. Broadway is a mostly white congregation, with black and biracial people throughout the congregation and its leadership. The congregation also has a strong contingent of GLBTQI people. On Sundays and throughout the week, low-income, high-income, and middle-income people all gather together at Broadway. It's a collection of folks that always makes me think, *This is what the realm of God looks like.*

We are, by the standard measures of Protestant church life, a successful, abundant church. The generosity of our congregation allows us to always comfortably meet our budget, and most years show our membership increasing, not declining.

Those are good measures of abundance. But over my thirty years of ministry—as associate pastor at Broadway for five and a half years, then for eleven and a half years as the pastor in South Bend, and then back to Broadway as senior pastor for the last fourteen years—I've become increasingly attuned to the other kinds of abundance that continue to flourish in the neighbors and neighborhoods surrounding us.

Bibliography

Alexander, Michelle. *The New Jim Crow: Mass Incarceration in the Age of Colorblindness*. New York: New Press, 2010.

Beatty, Paul. *The Sellout: A Novel*. New York: Farrar, Straus & Giroux, 2015.

Berry, Wendell. *Life Is a Miracle: An Essay against Modern Superstition*. Washington, D.C.: Counterpoint, 2000.

Bornstein, David. "When Families Lead Themselves Out of Poverty." *New York Times*, August 15, 2017.

Chacour, Elias. *Blood Brothers*. Grand Rapids: Chosen Books, 1984.

Clifton, Lucille. *The Collected Poems of Lucille Clifton*. Rochester, NY: BOA Editions Ltd., 1987.

Evans, Mari. *Continuum: New and Selected Poems*. Chicago: Just Us Publishers, 2015.

Hartman, Saidiya. "The Terrible Beauty of the Slum." In *Brick: A Literary Journal*, July 28, 2017. See https://brickmag.com/the-terrible-beauty-of-the-slum/.

Levertov, Denise. *A Door in the Hive*. New York: New Directions, 1989.

Maitland, Sara. *A Joyful Theology*. Minneapolis: Augsburg Press, 2002.

McKnight, John, and Peter Block. *The Abundant Community: Awakening the Power of Families and Neighborhoods*. Chicago: American Planning Association, 2012.

Miller, Mauricio L. *The Alternative: Most of What You Believe about Poverty Is Wrong*. Lulu Publishing Services, 2017.

Mullainathan, Sendhil, and Eldar Shafir. *Scarcity: The New Science of Having Less and How It Defines Our Lives*. New York: Henry Holt & Company, 2013.

Neumark, Heidi. *Breathing Space: A Spiritual Journey in the South Bronx*. Boston: Beacon Press, 2013.

Rothstein, Richard. *The Color of Law: A Forgotten History of How Our Government Desegregated America*. New York: Liveright Publishing Corporation, 2017.

Schaper, Donna. *A Book of Common Power: Narratives against the Current*. San Diego: Luramedia, 1989.

Wainaina, Binyavanga. *One Day I Will Write about This Place*. Lagos, Nigeria: Farafina, 2011.

Wells, Samuel. *A Nazareth Manifesto: Being with God*. Hoboken, NJ: Wiley, 2015.

Whitehead, Colson. *The Underground Railroad: A Novel*. New York: Doubleday, 2016.

Acknowledgments

Aren't there annunciations
of one sort or another
in most lives?

—Denise Levertov, "Annunciation"*

The annunciations I have received have come from more good folks than I deserve.

Thank you to the people of the parishes I have served, too many to name here, but including Parker Pengilly and Margaret Glass, Dick and Jo Nichols, Hertha Taylor, Clarissa Parks, Cindy and Mike Knaack, Scott Collins, Ann Pettifer, Peter Walshe, David Labrum, Ann Chernish, Bill and Emma McKinney, Mike Schaefer, Beth Ann Matar, Jeff Reed, Lyle West, Lige Fowler, Albert Hidalgo and Dan Hilton, Bill and Sue Ann Brown, Kate Singer and Ed Nichols, Vicki Kaser, Dolores Heaton, Frances Leath, Libby and Nick Buck, Ann Daly, and Carol and Gene Hoffman.

One of the laypeople who deserves much thanks is Seana Murphy. I met her in Indianapolis when she was seventeen, and

*Denise Levertov, "Annunciation," *A Door in the Hive* (New York: New Directions, 1989), 86.

we have spent the past thirty years in conversation. Seana's life and witness have fed a lot of the ideas and experiences I've written about in these pages.

In 1986 Dr. Philip Amerson asked me to join the staff of Broadway UMC in Indianapolis. Why he would do that I have no idea, but I'm grateful he did. For the next five-and-a-half years, he and the Rev. Mary Ann Moman taught me not only what to pay attention to, but to do it with humor and delight. Their constant inquiry, questioning, and support when I did crazy things helped me to realize what was possible, what I could see, and what I couldn't imagine otherwise.

The Rev. Dr. Vanessa Allen-Brown and the late Rev. Jicelyn Thomas shaped my life, faith, and ministry. I spent many, many late nights talking with them, arguing with them, and making plans with them.

When Dr. Craig Dykstra invited me to write a memoir, he threw me off my game. *Every preacher thinks they should write a memoir*, I thought to myself. But he persisted, and I'm grateful for the support of the Collegeville Institute and the Lilly Endowment. They invested in me and this project in ways that will continue to feed my life.

When I began this project, my friends Dr. Tamara Leech and Dr. Greg Ellison worked with me to figure out how to structure it so that I could communicate what I felt was important.

Thank you to readers John McKnight, Janel Bakker, Mike Green, Jonathan Wilson-Hartgrove, Rev. Felipe Martinez, Rev. Alan Rumble, Terry Muck, Rev. Deborah Coble, Dan Carpenter, Rev. Kevin Armstrong, Dan LeVay, the Reverends Grace and Taylor Burton-Edwards, and Don Richter.

I'm also grateful to my research assistant and friend, Rev. Fernando Rodriguez, who took great notes on books that I didn't have time to read and then had the patience to sit and talk with me about them, in ways that made me understand the world better—and also made me laugh. Thank you!

Acknowledgments

Thanks to Dr. Lauren Winner for editing and encouraging me in the final steps of getting this book finished. Thanks to Beth Gaede, Jean Smith, and Kenneth Morgan, who spent painstaking hours working with me on how to organize and perfect this book. Jean served as my best cheerleader and editor of this work, and I'm grateful to her beyond measure. She has opened the world to me. Thank you to all of them.

Over the past ten years the Rev. Brian White, the Rev. Gary Schaar, the Rev. Jimmy Moore, and I have met once a month to commiserate and encourage one another in our lives and common work. An ecumenical gathering of clergy that included the Rev. Teri Thomas and the late Rev. Michael Jones always pushed me both in the writing of this book and in my willingness to risk for the sake of the gospel.

My thanks to Nomabelu Mvambo-Dandala and the people of the Diakonia Council of Churches in Durban, South Africa, for their hospitality to my family and me in July of 2007. This remarkable and history-making group challenged me to see how the church could be a helpful force in society and one's community beyond what I had thought was possible for institutions.

Two poets have fed the work of this book. Mari Evans, whom Maya Angelou called "the greatest living American poet," allowed me to visit with her every week. A regular parishioner at Broadway before becoming homebound, she challenged me to think not only about words and the discipline of writing, but also about race and economy and its role in our lives and in the church. Poet and teacher Fran Quinn spent days with me at the beginning of this project reminding me that everything I write has two voices: "the voice of the poet and the voice of the poem." I've listened hard to hear the voice of what I've been writing. I hope I got it.

For many years I wrote e-mails to my friends telling them stories about what was happening in front of me. Dr. Elaine Amerson saved those stories and encouraged me to keep telling them, so that I could tell them to you.

For the past fourteen years I have worked alongside the Rev. Dr. Rachel Metheny, who is an exceptionally fine pastor and who continues to bless me with her hard work, imagination, and willingness to do my work when I'm away writing. (She does this so well that when I return, people say, "Oh, were you gone?") Rachel has been co-pastor, my friend, my most constant teacher, and my most impatient reader ("Can you get this thing done?"). Thank you.

Thanks to my friend the Rev. Karen "Vashti" Lang, who remains one of the most courageous people I know in ministry today—who loves the city and loves her calling and will not be deterred.

My friend De'Amon Harges is a genius when it comes to community. The way he lives his life and the work he does continue to inspire and push me to think more creatively and risk more courageously to try to keep up with him.

Thanks to my friends Lynne Butler and John Hicks, who opened their home in the mountains to me, so I might listen more carefully to what this book was teaching me.

Thanks to my in-laws, Bob and Judy Licht, for offering the gracious hospitality of their home on Clear Lake in Three Rivers, Michigan, where I could read and write and find the rest necessary for a full and generous life.

My first pastor was my father—the Rev. Herb Mather. He and my mother, Lillian Mather, formed me in innumerable important ways. Dad was an early and frequent reader of this text, and his insight and honesty have helped me tremendously. My brothers and sister—Pete, Alan, and Linda, each living in very different ways and settings—caused me to re-think the approaches I use in my work. Thank you.

My wife Kathy, and our sons, Conor and Jordan, have been my greatest teachers. Kathy has been especially patient, quietly encouraging, and graciously loving through this whole project. Conor and Jordan have reminded me over and over again about the joy and diversity there is even in families that look a lot alike. They are a reminder of the preciousness of all of life.